The Literature of Virginia in the Seventeenth Century

THE LITERATURE OF VIRGINIA IN THE SEVENTEENTH CENTURY

HOWARD MUMFORD JONES
WITH THE AID OF
SUE BONNER WALCUTT

SECOND EDITION

UNIVERSITY PRESS OF VIRGINIA
CHARLOTTESVILLE

The University Press of Virginia
Second edition, © 1968 by the Rector and
Visitors of the University of Virginia
First edition, Copyright, 1946 by Howard
Mumford Jones

Second edition first published 1968

Library of Congress
Catalog Card Number: 68–24630
Printed in the
United States of America

PREFATORY NOTE

THIS monograph was originally published in 1946 as one of the *Memoirs* of the American Academy of Arts and Sciences. This revised edition takes account of material that has come to hand since that time and corrects errors in the first edition. The original author gratefully acknowledges the help of Sue Bonner Walcutt in preparing this revision.

HOWARD MUMFORD JONES

Cambridge, Massachusetts
1967

CONTENTS

ILLUSTRATIONS

The Literature of Virginia in the Seventeenth Century

1. THE GENERAL MOVEMENT OF PROSE

T O SPEAK OF THE LITERARY LIFE OF SEVENTEENTH-CENTURY VIRGINIA, IF BY "LITERARY" ONE IMPLIES BELLES LETTRES, IS IN ONE SENSE LUDICROUS, BUT IN another sense that colony not only produced a surprising amount of writing but was also the cause of literature in others. Before Plymouth and Massachusetts Bay the Jamestown settlement regarded itself as a providential fact of highest consequence in its own time and of historical significance for generations to come. It did not fail to record its own annals. The first ships returning to England—the *Sarah Constant* and the *Godspeed*—as a Virginia historian points out, carried a literary cargo as well as samples of the natural products of the country. That budget of manuscripts included "A report of His Majesties Counsel for the first Colony [in] Virginia to His Majesties Counsel for Virginia in England"; *A relatyon of the Discovery* by "A Gentleman of the Colony" (presumably Gabriel Archer) ; Robert Tindall's "dearnall of our voyage," which has disappeared; a letter from Tindall to the Prince of Wales; one from

George Percy to a Mr. Warner; one from a Dutchman to John Pory (in Latin), and one from William
Brewster to the Earl of Salisbury,[1] besides other material not now identifiable. Within a decade of its
founding, a dozen or so pamphlets or treatises on the
infant enterprise had been penned, histories had been
written, and a variety of letters (a Jacobean letter
was usually a serious affair) had described Virginian
life. Also the rudiments of a literature of political
theory existed *in posse,* if not *in esse.* This represents
literary activity so out of proportion to the population as to suggest that "Virginia Britannia" was regarded as something novel in English history; and in
fact the same sense of divine significance which led
the Mathers to record "providences" overhung
Jamestown.[2] The providential "note" of the sermon
preached before Lord de la Warr when he landed
may be gleaned from its text, and the providential
note is characteristic:

Now the Lord had said unto Abram, Get thee out
of thy country, and from thy kindred, and from thy
father's house, unto a land that I will shew thee. And
I will make of thee a great nation . . . and in thee
shall all families of the earth be blessed.[3]

[1] Matthew Page Andrews, *Virginia: The Old Dominion* (New
York, 1937), p. 28.

[2] Thus in his *Historie of Travaile into Virginia Britannia* (ed.
R. H. Major for the Hakluyt Society; London, 1849) William
Strachey attributes the persistence of the English in settling Virginia
to "the will of the Eternall Wisdome, and so let all Christian and
charitable hearted believe in compassion to this people [i.e., the na-
tives]" (p. 153). And John Smith in the *Trve Relation* of 1608 (his
first published work) writes that "400. Indians the day before had
assalted the fort, and supprised it, had not God (beyond al their ex-
pectations) by meanes of the shippes (at whom they shot with their
Ordinances and Muskets) caused them to retire" (*Travels and
Works,* ed. Arber-Bradley [Edinburgh, 1910], I, 7).

[3] Andrews, *op. cit.,* p. 55.

During the formative years the proportion of gentlemen with some tincture of letters seems to have been unusually high for a wilderness settlement. Not to speak of John Smith and George Sandys,[4] Jamestown early saw such educated ministers as the Rev. Robert Hunt, who lost his library in the colony, the Rev. Mr. Poole, the Rev. William Mays (or Mease) at Kecoughtan, the Rev. Richard Bucke ("a verie good preacher"), the Rev. William Wickham of Henrico, whose "life and doctrine give good examples and godly instruction," and the better known Rev. William Whitaker, graduate of St. John's College, Cambridge, who baptized Pocahontas. When Lord de la Warr died, the colony counted among its mem-

[4] Sandys's translation of Ovid was first published in London in 1626; an earlier (1621?) printing of the first five books, long thought to be apocryphal or pirated, has at length been verified (James G. McManaway, "The First Five Bookes of Ovids Metamorphosis, 1621, Englished by Master George Sandys," *Papers of the Bibilographical Society, University of Virginia*, I [1948–49], 71–82). The remaining books were translated either on shipboard or during Sandys's residence in Virginia from 1621 to 1625. Vigorous claims that this translation should be counted among American literary masterpieces have been urged from Moses Coit Tyler downward, and it is true that in his dedication to Charles I the poet claims his work was "bred in the New World," a statement of course not true of the first five books. That there is an American interest in this translation is clear, but I think the earlier statement by Richard Beale Davis that "America's part in this first example of *belles lettres* is almost purely incidental" ("Early Editions of George Sandys's 'Ovid': The Circumstances of Production," *Papers of the Bibliographical Society of America*, XXXV [1941], 255–276) is sounder than his later claim ("America in George Sandys's 'Ovid,'" *William and Mary Quarterly*, 3d ser., IV [1947], 297–304) that Sandys's verses are "no more . . . un-American . . . than those of Edward Taylor or Anne Bradstreet." Surely there is a distinction between writing in America and American writing, and a poet who brings a translation more than one-third done to the New World and there finishes it offers no good parallel to, say, Captain John Smith. But see Davis' admirable *George Sandys: Poet-Adventurer* (London, 1955).

bers George Thorpe, M.P., a member of the privy council; William Strachey the historian; John Pory, M.P., letter writer, translator, and historian; William Claiborne; Captain Francis West (brother of de la Warr); Dr. John Pott; John Rolfe; Ralph Hamor; and George Sandys. Inasmuch as the total population was about two thousand, the percentage of "literary" men is remarkable; and, moreover, literary competency among the small governing group seems to have been common enough, if the following letter from Captain Peter Wynne is representative:

Most noble knight

I was not so desirous to come into this Country, as I am now willing here to end my dayes: for I finde it a farr more pleasant, and plentifull country than any report made mencon of upon the River wch wee are seated I have gon six or seaven score miles, and so farr is navigable; afterward I travailed between 50 or 60 myles by land, into a Country Called Monacon who owe no subiection to Powaton; this Land is very high ground and fertill, being very full of very delicate springes of sweet water: the ayre more helthfull than the place wher wee are seated, by reason it is not subiect to such fogges and mistes as we continually have. the people of Monacon speak a farr differing Language from the subiectes of Powaton, theyr pronunciation Being very like welch so that the gentlemen in o^r Company desired me to be theyr Interpretor. The Comodities as yet knowne in this Country wherof ther wilbe great store, is Pitch, Tarr, Sope ashes, and some dyes, wherof we have sent examples. As for thinges more p^{r}cious I omit till tyme (wch I hope wilbe shortly) shall make manifest proof of it. As concerning yor request of Bloudhoundes, I cannot Learne that ther is any such in this Country; only the dogges wch are here are a Certeyne kind of Currs like o^r wariners hey dogges in England; and they keep

them to hunt theyr land fowles, as Turkeys and such
like, for they keep nothing tame about them. hereaf-
ter I doubt not but to give you at Large a farther
relacon then as yet I am able to doe, and doe therfore
desire you to take theis fewe Lines in good part and
hold me excused for the rest untill ffitter oportunity.
Thus Comending my service to yor good Love wth
many thankes for all favours and kindnesses received
from you I doe ever remayne

yo^{rs} most devoted in all service
Peter wyn

JAMES TOWNE in VIRGINIA
this XXVI of NOVEMBER [?1608] [5]

Obviously a settlement containing a settler who
compares Indian dialects with the Welsh language
and who writes this easy prose was far different in
its cultural outlook from, let us say, an American
frontier town two hundred years later.

The necessity of establishing the general literary
level of the tiny but influential upper class in seventeenth-century Virginia arises from a natural inclina-
tion among historians, bemused by the extraordinary
production of printed matter in New England, to
look upon Captain John Smith as a sport plant in an
unliterary wilderness. That the quantity of "literature" produced in Virginia is far less than that in
Massachusetts is patent, but something depends upon
what one means by "literature" and something depends also upon what one means by a culture group.
The Virginians were neither unlettered nor indifferent to books. Recent investigations reveal that the
first settlers brought books with them, that the libraries of the larger plantations contained volumes

[5] Printed by Andrews, *op. cit.,* pp. 39–40, from a MS in the Hunting-
ton Library.

collected for piety, utility, learning, and leisure, and
that even the smaller farm might have its small shelf
of books.[6] Seventeenth-century correspondence is another gauge of literary cultivation, and it is clear that
Virginia letters, so far as they have been printed,
spring out of a common cultural inheritance.[7] Another gauge is the English of the public records.

Whether the *Lavves Diuine, Morall and Martiall*
for the *"Colony in Virginea Britannia"* as published
by Strachey in 1612 [8] is "literature" or no, it sets a

[6] See *inter alia* George K. Smart, "Private Libraries in Colonial
Virginia," *American Literature,* X (1938), 24–52; and Louis B.
Wright, *The First Gentlemen of Virginia: Intellectual Qualities of
the Early Colonial Ruling Class* (San Marino, Calif., 1940; reprinted
Charlottesville, Va., 1964) which sums up a number of earlier articles by this scholar. On the origins of the ruling class and their English connections consult chapters iii–vi of Philip Alexander Bruce,
Social Life of Virginia in the Seventeenth Century (Richmond, 1907).
"The community," writes Bruce, "from a social point of view, was as
if some shire of England, with its whole population, had been moved
bodily over sea" (p. 104).

[7] Although concern for education was sporadic and although most
of the projects did not come to fruition, Wright concludes after a survey of Virginian interest in education that "a gentleman did not need
the education of a pedant, but . . . his position required him to know
how to speak and write good English, to be a competent penman, and
to have command of enough mathematics to qualify him to manage
his accounts and deal with simple problems in surveying. In general
it was incumbent upon him to acquire sufficient knowledge to enable
him to be intelligent in whatever company he found himself. Latin
was still generally believed to be eminently useful—a sort of key to
other forms of learning. The gentleman's schooling should give him
the kind of training that would fit him to continue his studies after
his formal education was finished" (*op. cit.,* p. 115). It may be
doubted whether there was much real command of Latin among the
plantation owners, but the emphasis upon "good English" is certainly
important.

[8] Reprinted in Peter Force, comp., *Tracts and Other Papers* (Washington, 1836–46), Vol. III, no. 2, and photostatically reproduced by
the Massachusetts Historical Society in *Photostat Americana,* 2d ser.,
no. 16 (Boston, 1936), from the original edition. Quotations in the
text are from the latter.

distinguished standard. Few legal codes have been prefaced by a sonnet; few have been written in such direct and easy prose. Consider, for example, this passage from a preamble to the regulations concerning the governor:

If the wisest man that euer spake or writ (except him that was both God & man) summed vp all the reckonings of worldly felicities in these two words *Laetari & benefacere,* imploying a cheereful mirth with well doing (from which it cannot be seuered) who hath more cause to be cheerefull, and inlie glad then you that haue the comfort of so great weldoing, to which no other may be compared? for what weldoing can be greater then to be stocks & authors of a people that shal serue and glorifie God . . . & to redeeme thē from ignorance and infidelity, to the true knowledge and worship of God (p. 36).

A solemn dedication of themselves to Divine Providence was enjoined both upon the civil part of the colonists:

Likewise no man or woman shall dare to violate or breake the Sabboth by any gaming, publique, or priuate abroad, or at home, but duly sanctifie and obserue the same, both himselfe and his familie, by preparing themselues at home with priuate prayer . . . as also euery man and woman shal repaire in the morning to the diuine service, and Sermons preached vpon the Saboth day, and in the afternoon to diuine seruice, and Catechising (p. 4);

and upon the military, whose officers "shall make their publike and faithfull prayers, vnto almighty God for his blessing and protection to attend them . . . the whole day," remembering

how that first & great commander ouer the Colony of the children of Israel, conducting them from Ægypt to make their plantation in the land of Promise, appointed Captains ouer Tribes and hundreds for the wars, and Elders to sit vpon the bench (p. 47).

Strachey was, of course the most distinguished "author" in the colony next to Smith, but lest it be thought that his pamphlet of laws is a special case, let us turn elsewhere.

The publication of the *Journals of the House of Burgesses of Virginia, 1619–1658/59* [9] and of the succeeding volume for 1659/60–1693 enables one to survey the whole development of English style for public purposes during the century. The minutes of the house were written in better fashion from 1619 to the middle of the century than during the rest of the period. The excellence of the first entries is, of course, due to the skill of John Pory, who "wrote up" his "A Reporte of the Manner of Proceeding in the General Assembly Convented at James Citty in Virginia, July 30 1619" in the grand historical manner:

> The most convenient place we could finde to sitt in was the Quire of the Churche, Where Sir *George Yeardley* the Governour being sett downe in his accustomed place, those of the Counsel of Estate sate nexte him on both handes excepte onely the Secretary then appointed Speaker, who sate right before him; *John Twine* clerke of the General Assembly being placed nexte the Speaker and *Thomas Pierse* the Sergeant standing at the barre, to be ready for any service the Assembly should comand him. But for as muche as mens affaires doe little prosper where Gods service is neglected; all the Burgesses took their places in the Quire, till a Prayer was said by Mr *Bucke,* the Minister, that it would please God to

[9] Ed. H. R. McIlwaine (Richmond, 1915). The volume for 1659/60–1693 under the same editorship was printed in 1914.

guide us & sanctifie all our proceedings to his owne
glory, and the good of this Plantation, Prayer being
ended, to the intente that as wee had begun at God
Almighty soe wee might proceed wth awful and due
respecte towards his Lieutenant, our most gratious &
dread Soveraigne, all the Burgesses were intreated to
retyre themselves into the body of the Churche; w^{ch}
being done, before they were fully admitted, they
were called in order & by name, & so every man
(none staggering at it) tooke the oathe of Supremacy,
& then entered the Assembly.[10]

This is good prose in any period of literary history,
but lest it be thought that Pory gives a false impression of legislative excellence, note the fierce realism
and graphic detail of a later "answere of the Generall Assembly in *Virginia* to a Declaration of the
state of the Colonie in the 12 yeers of Sr *Thomas
Smiths* Gouerment, exhibited by Alderman *Johnson*
and others," with which Pory presumably had less to
do:

The allowance in those tymes for a man was only
eight ounces of meale and half a pinte of pease for a
daye the one & ye other mouldy, rotten, full of Cob-
webs and Maggots loathsome to man and not fytt for
beasts, wch forced many to flee for reliefe to the Savage Enemy, who being taken againe, were putt to
sundry deaths as by hanginge, shootinge and break-
inge uppon the wheele & others were forced by famine to filch for their bellies, of whom one for steelinge
2 or 3 pints of oatmeale had a bodkinge thrust
through his tongue and was tyed wth a chaine to a tree
untill he starued, yf a man through his sickness had
not been able to worke, he had no allowance at all,
and so consequently perished many through these ex-

[10] *Journals*, I, 4. Pory's report is also reprinted in *Narratives of
Early Virginia, 1606–1625,* ed. L. G. Tyler (Original Narratives of
Early American History; New York, 1907), pp. 249–278.

tremities, being weery of life digged holes in the earth and hidd themselues till they famished.[11]

Four years later the colony sent to England a document which contains so well-turned a cadence as this:

> But notw[th]standing wee have continually beene insnared in these toyles, and for these six yeares have perpetually laboured in the confused pathes of those labyrinthes, being rather framed and built in the very imaginacon of unconscionable and unjust men, then uppon good and sound reason or w[th] any respecte to the benefitt and advancem[t] of the Colony . . .[12]

Such a passage implies a good ear for prose.

To be sure, the amplitude and splendor of Jacobean style degenerated as less cultured colonists of the next generation struggled with the language,[13] yet in the fifties Governor Berkeley was capable of plain, straightforward eloquence:

> Consider your selves how happy you are and have been, how the Gates of wealth and Honour are shut on no man, and that there is not here an Arbitrary hand that dares to touch the substance of either poore or rich: But that which I woud have you chiefly consider with thankfullnes is: That God hath seperated you from the guilt of the crying bloud of

[11] *Journals,* I, 21; and see also Tyler, *op. cit.,* 412–418; 422–426. This is from the official records for 1623/24. McIlwaine of course prints from manuscript without alteration. Had a Jacobean printer "set up" this material he would have edited it, so that the run-on sentences would not have been left as they are.

[12] *Journals,* I, 45. "The humble Answer of the Governo[r] & Counsell together wth the Burgesses of the severall Plantations assembled in *Virginia* unto his Ma[ts] Letter concerning our Tobaccoe and other Comodities," March 26, 1628.

[13] One notes by reading the *Journals* a slow decline in command of prose during the late thirties. A document from the burgesses to the governor and council of 1637/38 employs 351 words in its second sentence. *Ibid.,* pp. 62–63.

our Pious Souveraigne of ever blessed memory: . . .
what is it can be hoped for in a change, which we
have not allready? Is it liberty? The sun looks not on
a people more free then we are from all oppression.
Is it wealth? Hundreds of examples shew us that Industry & Thrift in a short time may bring us to as
high a degree of it, as the Country and our Condi-
tions are yet capable of: Is it securety to enjoy this
wealth when gotten? With out blushing I will speake
it, I am confident theare lives not that person can ac-
cuse me of attempting the least act against any mans
property. Is it peace? The Indians, God be blessed
round about us are subdued; we can onely feare the
Londoners.[14]

In the second half of the period the records settle
upon a perspicuous but unexciting legal style. It cannot be denied that the general level of this prose is
lower in 1680 than was the prose of the founders, or
that attempts to make it "literary" were sometimes
distressing.[15] The absence of a printing press helps to
explain why prose like other arts tended to become
coarse-fibered, but it must also be noted that degenera-
tion did not wholly set in, and that the presence of
royal commissioners and the coming of new and accomplished governors helped to maintain stylistic stand-
ards. Thus from a Royal Commission sent out after
the Bacon Rebellion comes language like this:

[14] "Speech of Sir *Wm. Berkeley,*" *ibid.,* pp. 75–76.

[15] The address of the burgesses to Sir Henry Chicheley and the
council April 19, 1682, is filled with verbose phrases like "our most
dread and most gratious Soueraignes," "most humble and loyall Subjects," "ouerwhelmed and oppressed with greife," "dolefull & most
pierceing apprehensions, and fears," "sweet assureances of his Maties
& yor hono^rs superlatiue grace and goodness." Aside from the amusing sycophancy, one notes that the members of these double construc-
tions do not strengthen each other. *Ibid.,* II, 158–159.

And for that in considerate sort of men, who soe rashly and Causelesly cry up a Warr and seeme to wish and ayme att an utter extirpation of the Indians (and are yett the first that Complayne and murmur att the charge and taxes that on any just occasion attends such a Warr) Wee would wish such to lay their hands on their hearts and seriously Consider with themselves whither it bee not a base Ingratitude, a namelesse Prodigie of Infatuation and neer madnesse in such men, as would make a breach with or strive to destroy and Extirpate those Amicable Indians (who are soe farr from hurting them or us) that wee must justly confesse they are our best Guards to secure us on the ffrontiers from the Incursions and suddaine Assaults of those more barbarous Indians of the Continent, who never can bee brought to keepe a Peace with us, but will still continue our most implacable and mortall enemies and the more their dayly Murders and depredations are upon us, the more earnestly it inforces this Argument for a Peace with the frontier Indians.[16]

The addresses of the governors must on the whole have maintained a level of dignity and grace.[17] The letters of the period, it will also be seen, attain a certain excellence.[18] Because the formal literary production of the Virginians was small, it should not be inferred that the upper class was lacking in a graceful literary culture.

[16] *Ibid.,* pp. 91–92.

[17] Lord Culpeper's address is the earliest gubernatorial address yet found (*ibid.,* pp. xxi, 147–149). It is to be feared that his lordship was not at ease with a pen in his hand, but we do not know that his is a representative case, and from fragments of prose by other administrators it would appear that he was not.

[18] See below, pp. 72–85.

2. THE LITERATURE OF EXPLORATION AND SETTLEMENT: THE LESSER WRITERS

AGAINST THESE HISTORICAL OBSER-
VATIONS MUST NOW BE PRO-
JECTED THE INDIVIDUAL WORKS
WHICH CONSTITUTE THE LITER-
ATURE OF VIRGINIA IN THE SEVEN-
teenth century. What were these writings? If one
begins American literature with material dealing with
the first permanent English settlement on the Atlantic
seaboard, primacy must go to Master George Percy,
brother of the Earl of Northumberland and on two
occasions governor of the colony, whose "Observations gathered out of a Discourse of the Plantation of
the Southerne Colonie in Virginia by the English,
1606" is in point of time the earliest account of the
Jamestown settlement by one who participated in it.[1]

[1] Earliest in the sense that it covers the setting out of the expedition
and the crossing of the ocean.

George Percy was a son of the eighth Earl of Northumberland and
of Catherine, his wife, daughter of Lord Latimer. He was born September 4, 1580; served in youth as a soldier in the Low Countries;
sailed for Virginia in December, 1606; and was among the incorporators of the second Virginia Company. After the recall of John
Smith (September, 1609) he served as deputy governor during the
"starving time" until the arrival of Sir Thomas Gates in May, 1610.
He served again briefly in the spring of 1611, but left for England in

It is, however, impossible to judge Percy on the basis
of the "Observations" alone because Purchas not only
cut short the account but tampered with the style. This
editorial clumsiness leaves an ill-porportioned narrative which, just as it reaches the tragic "starving
time," dwindles into chronology. In the "Observations" Percy gives an occasional personal impression,
as when he writes that he was "almost ravished" at
the first sight of the "faire meddowes and goodly tall
Trees, with . . . Fresh-waters running through the
woods," or when he says he observed an Indian
dance, but for the most part his account (as edited)
is impersonal. He had, however, a good eye for
detail, as when he describes the Kecoughtan savages

April, 1612. In 1625 he volunteered for service against Spain in the
Low Countries, where in 1627 he commanded a company. He died in
1632. See the biography by C. R. Beazley in *DNB;* that by Armistead
Churchill Gordon, Jr., in *DAB,* and John W. Shirley, "George Percy
at Jamestown, 1607–1612" *Virginia Magazine of History and Biography,* LVII (1949), 227–243.

The original manuscript from which Purchas took his abridgment,
"Observations gathered out of a Discourse of the Plantation of the
Southerne Colonie in Virginia by the English, 1606," has disappeared. All that remains is the abridgment published by Purchas in
Hakluytus Posthumus, or Pvrchas His Pilgrimes (London, 1625). In
the edition of Purchas published at Glasgow by James MacLehose
and Sons, 1905–6, in 20 volumes, the Percy material is in XVIII, 403–
419. It has been reprinted also in Tyler's *Narratives of Early Virginia,* pp. 5–23, and in the Arber-Bradley edition of Captain John
Smith, I, lvii–lxxiii. It has recently been edited by David B. Quinn and
published in a somewhat modernized version for the Association for
the Preservation of Virginia Antiquities in its Jamestown Documents
series (Charlottesville, Va., 1967). "A Trewe Relacyon of the Pro-
cedeinges and Ocurrentes of Momente wch have hapned in Virginia
from the Tyme Sr Thomas GATES was shippwrackte uppon the BER-
MUDES an° 1609 untill my depture outt of the Country wch was in an°
Dñi 1612" was first printed in *Tyler's Quarterly Historical and Gen-
ealogical Magazine,* III (1922), 260–282.

swimming a river with "Bowes and Arrowes in their mouthes," or pictures a flute-playing "Werowance" whose

body was painted all with Crimson, with a Chaine of Beads about his necke, his face painted blew, be-sprinkled with silver Ore as wee thought, his eares all behung with Braslets of Pearle, and in either eare a Birds Claw through it beset with fine Copper or Gold.

This in its way is as good as White's drawings. The descendant of Harry Hotspur gazed with respect upon this specimen of barbaric dignity:

He entertained us in so modest a proud fashion, as though he had beene a Prince of civill government, holding his countenance without laughter or any such ill behaviour.

Yet, despite episodes of some dramatic vigor,[2] the "Observations" is incurious about cause and effect, so that the reader is suddenly thrust out of a "Paradise" "flowing over with faire flowers of sundry colours and kindes" into a catalogue of deaths due to a "bloudie Fluxe" and the horrors of starvation, for which Percy does nothing to prepare him.

These form a substantial portion of a grimmer narrative, Percy's "Trewe Relacyon," written some years after the "Observations." Addressed to the author's brother, the ninth Earl of Northumberland, this is a defense of Percy's American career against an anonymous "Auther" (? Smith), who "hathe nott Spared to Apropriate many desertts to himselfe w^ch

---

[2] Percy had some sense of the larger historical significance of at least one episode, in which an Indian vainly shot arrows, which broke against a steel "Target" set against a tree, then bit his remaining arrows in rage and departed in anger.

he never pformd." This document [3] has great human
interest, whatever its historical bias. Excepting Wingfield's *Discourse,* no other history brings us more
closely in touch with the brave, mercurial, unhappy,
and very fallible human beings who created the
Jamestown settlement. The author's malevolence is
evident, but it gives us the very form and pressure of
the time:

Shorttly after Capte: SMITHE sente Capteyne
Francis WEST wᵗʰ one hundrethe and fortye men
upp to the falles wᵗʰ six monthes victewells to in-
habitt there. Where beinge Reasonable well settled
dyv[ers] of his men stragled from their foarte. some
of them comeinge hoame wownded. others never returned to bringe any Tydeings butt weare cutt of and
slayne by the salvages. So that in small [pro]cesse of
Tyme Capteyne SMITHE did take his iorney upp to
the falles to understand how things weare there ordered when presently after his comeinge thether A
great devisyon did growe amongste them Capte:
SMITHE [per]ceaveinge bothe his authorety and
[per]son neglected incensed and Animated the Salvages agenste Capte: West and his company Re-
porteinge unto them thatt our men had noe more
powder lefte them then wolde serve for one volley of
shott And so Capt: SMITHE Retour[n]inge to
JAMES TOWNE ageine fownd to have too

[3] Prior to the publication of the whole "Trewe Relacyon" by Tyler
in 1922, it was supposed that the "Observations" were taken from it
because in publishing a part of the "Trewe Relacyon" in his *Virginia
Vetusta* (Albany, 1885), E. D. Neill announced a gap in the manuscript from p. 3 to p. 38. He also hinted that the "Trewe Relacyon" is
an answer to Captain John Smith. These two points have been de-
bated at length: see *Virginia Magazine of History and Biography,*
I (1894), 473-476 (W. W. Henry); VI (1899), 329 (Alexander
Brown); XII (1905), 425-429 (Elmer I. Miller). Miller argued
acutely as early as 1905 that the two manuscripts must be independent.

mutche powder aboutt him The w°h being in his
pockett where the sparke of A Matche Lighted very
shrewdly burned him. And comeinge in thatt case to
JAMES TOWNE Capte RATTLIEFE ARCHER
and MARTIN practysed ageinste him and depos[d]
him of his governmentt SMITHE beinge an Am-
bityous unworthy and vayneglorious fellowe Attempt-
einge to take all Mens Authoreties from them . . .

Percy's satisfaction in the poetic justice of Smith's being burned by powder following his alleged treachery
about the powder supply connotes a streak of cruelty
in the Jacobean mind, the existence of which is confirmed by other passages. When seventeen mutineers
stole away in a boat, they were "in all lykelyhood
. . . Cutt of and slayne by the Salvages" "acordinge
to their desertts," says the implacable author. The
spectacle of the dead bodies of Ratcliffe [Sicklemore]
and others in the woods, "their mowthes stopped full
of Breade beinge donn as it seamethe in Contempte
and skorne," draws from him only a learned parallel
with the fate of a Spaniard. One paragraph, written
with the impersonality of a Flaubert, mounts to a
climax of weird evil:

And now famin begineinge to Looke gastely and
pale in every face thatt notheinge was spared to
mainteyne Lyfe and to doe those things w°h seame
incredible As to digge up dead corpses outt of
graves and to eate them and some have Licked upp
the Bloode w°h hathe fallen from their weake fel-
lowes And amongste the rest this was moste Lament-
able Thatt one of our Colline murdered his wyfe
Ripped the childe outt of her woambe and threw itt
into the River and after chopped the Mother in
pieces and salted her for his foode The same not
beinge discovered before he had eaten [par]te thereof for the w°h crewell and inhumane factt I aiudged

him to be executed the acknowledgm^t of the dede
beinge inforced from him by torture haveinge hunge
by the Thumbes w^{t}h weightes att his feete a quarter of an howere before he wolde confesse the same.

The imagination of Webster, though it could describe
them poetically, cannot surpass such horrors. Indeed,
Percy's "Relacyon" is invaluable in its revelation of
naïveté and religious faith. One Hugh Price, "being
pinched w^{t}h extreme famin," cried out in the market
place that there was no God, went out in the woods
that afternoon with a butcher, "A corpulentt fatt
man," and was slain, his bowels being torn out by
wolves, whereas the butcher, also shot to death and
lying not six yards away, was "altogether untouched."
Therein, says Percy, God "sheowd his iuste Judgment."

When the whites were suffering these tortures, it
was not to be expected that the original dream of
friendly relations between Indians and the English
would appeal. Sir Thomas Gates lured certain abo-
riginals to the seashore by ordering the "Taborer" to
play and dance, whereupon the English "putt fyve to
the sworde & wownded many others some of them
beinge after fownde in the woods w^{t}h Sutche extreor-
dinary Lardge and mortall wownds thatt itt seamed
strange they Cold flye so far." Percy boasts of a massacre of Indians at Paspahas town carried out by his
orders. When the soldiers returned to the beat of a
drum from the chase, a lieutenant brought in a
"queen," her children, and an Indian warrior, only to
be reproved. "I cawsed the Indians heade to be cutt
of," he says proudly, and, the soldiers murmuring because the woman and children were spared,

upon the same A Cowncell beinge called itt was
Agreed upon to putt the Children to deathe the w^{c}h

was effected by Throweinge them overboard and shot-
einge owtt their Braynes in the water yett for all this
Crewellty the Sowldiers weare nott well pleased.

The unfortunate mother was butchered by Captain
Davis, because, "haveinge seene so mutche Blood-
shedd . . . now in my Cowldbloode," says Percy, "I
desyred to see noe more." Not love but weariness
brought Percy to his singular defense. He records
everything with the same imperturbability—massa-
cres, gossip, famine, his own dreadful return voyage,
when the ship's drinking water grew "so stencheous
thatt onely washeinge my hands there w'h I cold nott
endure the sentt thereof." In its small way "A Trewe
Relacyon" is a masterpiece of disagreeable detail.

Contemporaneous with Percy's "Observations" is
the group of three manuscripts printed as "Capt.
Newport's Discoveries, Virginia. May [1607]" commonly attributed to Gabriel Archer.[4] The first and
longest of these is the diary of an expedition starting
out "with a perfect resolutyon not to returne, but either to finde the head of this ryver, the laake men-
tyoned by others heretofore, the sea againe, the
mountaynes Apalatsi, or some issue," but this, the

---

[4] First published in *Archaeologia Americana: Transactions and
Collections of the American Antiquarian Society*, IV (1860), 40–65
by Edward E. Hale, these manuscripts are: "A Relatyon of the Discovery of our River, from James Forte into the Maine; made by Capt.
Christopher Newport, and sincerely written and observed by a Gentleman of the Colony"; "The Description of the Now-Discovered
River and Country of Virginia; with the liklyhood of ensuing ritches,
by England's Ayd and Industry"; and "A Brief Description of the
People." Alexander Brown and William Green were the first to at-
tribute these documents to Archer.

The second of these papers was reprinted in *Virginia Magazine
of History and Biography*, XIV (1907), 373–378; the "Brief Description of the People" occupies pp. 376–378 as a subtopic. The first of
these was gathered into the Arber-Bradley edition of Smith, I, xl–lv.

first exploration inland from Jamestown, did not proceed beyond the present site of Richmond. The most
interesting entries have to do with the Indians, the author's description of "Queen Apumatec" being a de-
lectable piece of work:

> Assending a pretty hill, we sawe the queene of this
> country cominge in selfesame fashion of state as
> Pawatah or Arahatec; yea, rather with more maj-
> esty. She had an usher before her, who brought her
> to the matt prepared under a faire mulbery-tree;
> where she satt her downe by herselfe, with a stayed
> countenance. She would permitt none to stand or sitt
> neere her. She is a fatt, lustie, manly woman. She had
> much copper about her neck; a crownet of copper
> upon her hed. She had long, black haire, which
> hanged loose downe her back to her myddle; which
> only part was covered with a dcarc's skyn, and ells
> all naked. She had her woemen attending on her,
> adorned much like herselfe (save they wanted the
> copper). Here we had our accustomed eates, tobacco,
> and wellcome. Our captain presented her with guyfts
> liberally; whereupon shee cheered somewhat her
> countenance, and requested him to shoote off a peece;
> whereat (wee noted) she shewed not neere the like
> as Arahatec, though he be a goodly man.

Indeed, there is a frank acceptance of the Indians as
human beings in this document, which is refreshing.[5]
"The Description of the Now-Discovered River and
Country of Virginia" was perhaps the first account of
the country to reach England from Jamestown, and

[5] One interesting passage throws light on the means by which savage and explorer communicated with each other: "Navirans, with
being with us in our boate, had learned me so much of the languadg,
and was so excellently ingenious in signing out his meaning, that I
could make him understand me, and perceive him also wellny in any
thing." The second and third documents are, as it were, appendixes
to the journal.

is inevitably enthusiastic. The James River runs between "two fertile and fragrant banks," the Virginia watercourses "devide the salvage kingdomes in many places, and yeeld pleasant seates, in all the country over by moystening the frutefull mould," the fishing is wonderful, and even the "black fatt sandy mould," though "somewhat slymy in touch," is "sweet in savour." As to the Indians the narrator seems unable to make up his mind whether to admire the absolute control which their monarchs have over them or to deprecate their being "naturally given to trechery," howbeit, he honestly adds, "we could not finde it in our travell up the river, but rather a most kind and loving people."

Still another facet of Jamestown life is revealed by Edward Maria Wingfield's *A Discourse of Virginia,* apparently written in 1608, which paints the petty side of the enterprise.[6] Wingfield was a Roman Catholic gentleman of some cultivation, facts which ex-

---

[6] Edward Maria Wingfield, son of Thomas Wingfield and of his second wife, grandson of Sir Richard Wingfield, quondam Lord Deputy of Calais and godson of Queen Mary, was born ca. 1560. He served in the Low Countries and in Ireland; was one of the original incorporators of the first Virginia Company, and was the only one to sail with the first settlers. Appointed to the council at Jamestown, he was elected by them first president of Virginia (April 26, 1607), deposed September 10, imprisoned for some months, and sent home, arriving May 21, 1608. He died ca. 1613. See the lives by J. A. Doyle in *DNB* and Wesley Frank Craven in *DAB.*

A Discourse of Virginia was first published by Charles Deane in 1860 in the volume of *Archaeologia Americana* just cited (IV [1860], 67–103). A reprint of 100 copies from this printing was made in Boston in 1860. There are also reprints in the Arber-Bradley edition of Smith's *Travels and Works* (I, lxxiv–xci) and in the appendix to Marshall Wingfield, *A History of Caroline County, Virginia* (Richmond, 1924), pp, 496 ff. Quotations in the text are from the first edition.

plain both the charges of treason which he rebuts in the "Finis" of his defense and his easy references to Cadmus, Romulus and Remus, and Amphion, but this well-bred delicacy unfitted him for the control of a colony filled with charges of treason, mutiny, and profiteering. His manuscript was left in an even less finished state than was Percy's: an unsigned foreword "in a different hand from the rest" is written in one style; the body of the narrative breaks in two as Wingfield shifts from the third person to the first; and the "Finis," which is both sad and comic in its littleness and humility, is in yet another vein. Wingfield writes not as a participant in great events, but as one to whom the deeds of more daring spirits have been imperfectly reported. His own comments on the "government" of the little colony are often those of a weak formalist, as when he told Ratcliffe and the council that the proceedings against him "ought to be verball" and "desired a coppie of the articles and tyme giuen me to answere them likewise by wrighting." He makes vague and unsupported charges against his enemies, but what most strikes the modern reader is the childish occasion of these quarrels:

It is further said, I did much banquit and ryot. I never had but one squirell roasted; whereof I gave part to Mr Ratcliff, then sick: yet was that squirell given me. I did never heate a flesh pott but when the comon pot was so used likewise.

A squirrel, a "whittle" or small pocketknife, a copper kettle—upon these trivial objects hung the future United States! Wingfield thus defends himself:

As truly as God liveth, I gave an ould man, then the keeper of the private stoure, 2 glasses wth sallet oyle wch I brought wth me out of England for my pri-

vate stoare, and willed him to bury it in the ground,
for that I feared the greate heate would spoile it.
Whatsoeuer was more, I did never consent vnto or
knewe of it; and as truly was it protested vnto me,
that all the remaynder before menčoned of the oyle,
wyne, &c, wch the President [Ratcliffe] receyued of
me when I was deposed, they themselues poored into
their owne bellyes.

.   .   .   .   .

To the President's and Councell's obiections I saie,
that I doe knowe curtesey and civility became a governor. . . .

. . . I [pro]test, my greatest contenčon was to
p°vent contenčon, and my chiefest endeavour to
p°serue the liues of others, though wth great hazard of
my own; for I neuer desired to enamell my name w^{th}
bloude.

Jamestown was no place for a humanist who did not
desire to enamel his name with blood, and Wingfield
seems an exotic plant among such hard-bitten figures
as Smith, Newport, Archer, and George Percy.

Of tougher breed, Henry Spelman [7] wrote a worse

---

[7] Son of Erasmus Spelman and nephew of Sir Henry Spelman the
antiquary, Henry Spelman was baptized in 1595(?) and came to Virginia in August, 1609, when he was sold to the Indians in exchange
for a town. Rescued by Captain Argall in December, 1610, he returned to England with Lord de la Warr in March, 1611. Back in
Virginia, he was employed as an interpreter and made a captain,
losing that rank in August, 1619, when the burgesses found him guilty
of disparaging Governor Yardley to the Indians. In 1623 he was
murdered by them. The only formal biographical sketch is in Alexander Brown, *The Genesis of the United States* (Boston and New York,
1890), II, 1020–1021, incorrect in certain details. This Henry Spelman was *not* the third son of Sir Henry: see the will of Francis
Saunder in *Virginia Magazine of History and Biography,* XV (1908),
305–306; but see in the same periodical II (1894), 65, and VI (1899),
242, and A. J. Morrison, "The Virginia Indian Trade to 1673," *William and Mary College Quarterly,* 2d ser., I (1921), 221–222.
    Edited by James F. Hunnewell, *The Relation of Virginea* was first

account, mostly intended to "giue sum satisfaction to my frends and contentment unto others" about his life among the savages. The first quarter of his manuscript relates his own adventures and includes two versions of an escape from "Kinge Patomecke"; the rest concerns his Indian existence. As Spelman was only fourteen or fifteen at the time, the chief interest of his account lies in his observations on Indian customs. These are seldom penetrating, the three most striking passages having to do with aboriginal marriage customs, the ceremonial cultivation of the soil, and barbarian warfare. Spelman has nothing much to say about this last except to make the curious comparison of a canoe to a "Hoggs trowgh," but his account of Indian family life is enlivened by a personal anecdote which approaches mediaeval farce. When he once refused to carry the child of an Indian woman,

she strook me 3 or 4 blows, but I beinge loith to bear to much gott to hir and puld hir doune giuing hir sum blows agayne which yᵉ other of yᵉ Kings wiues perseyuinge, they both fell on me beatinge me so as I thought they had lamd me.

When the "king" came home and laid out one wife with "a kind of paringe Iron," young Spelman fled to "a Neyghburs house, for feare of yᵉ Kings displeasuer," but the lady bore him no grudge, the monarch visited him next morning, and "I being by his speeches sumwhat boulder, Asked him for his Queene." Despite the fact that Smith thought Spelman "one of the best Interpreters in the Land," he

---

published in an edition of 50 (*not* 100) copies in London, 1872. It is reprinted in the Arber-Bradley edition of Smith, I, ci–cxiv, the text of which differs slightly from that of Hunnewell. The Arber-Bradley text is cited here.

was treacherously murdered by the savages whom he trusted and despised—reporting an Indian battle, for example, he remarks sarcastically that there was "no greater slawter of nether side."

These accounts are informal, but *The Proceedings of the English Colonie in Virginia* (Oxford, 1612), which forms the second part of John Smith's *A Map of Virginia,*[8] though coming from nine contributors, is a carefully articulated narrative, despite some stylistic variance, designed to illustrate the epic virtues of Captain Smith. The word "epic" throws a flood of light upon the structure of the work, which is in twelve books and which narrates the fortunes of two nations opposed in peace and war. The figure of Æneas-Smith, the transplanter to new shores of a wandering, yet divinely guided people, is dramatically contrasted with that of Powhatan, and both are sketched in grand and simple outline. Each hero is surrounded by lesser heroes and weaker men; each nation appeals to its own deities, the Christian God proving the stronger; appropriate orations on friendship, political power, the nature of greatness, authority, and ethics are uttered on both sides; and there are speeches of defiance and of "pollicie." The narrative

---

[8] *The Proceedings of the English Colonie in Virginia* was compiled by Richard Pots (Potts) from narratives written by Nathaniel Powell, Thomas Studlye, William Phettiplace, Dr. Walter Russell, Richard Wiffin, Thomas Abbey, Anas Todkill, Thomas Hope, and Pots himself. This manuscript was then apparently revised by the Rev. William Simmonds before publication, to whose learning and tact the unity and polish of the pamphlet are presumably much indebted. The work is readily available in the Arber-Bradley edition of Smith's *Travels and Works,* I, 85–174, albeit the editors have miscounted the contributors. The writers were Jamestown colonists, and the *Proceedings* and *A Map of Virginia* are sometimes referred to as the Oxford tract or tracts.

is single and whole; and the Christian hero, wily in diplomacy, skilled as an orator, ruler, warrior, lawgiver, a man above ordinary passions (Pocahontas was "the very Nomparell" of Powhatan's kingdom, but Smith "ever much respected" her, though "if he would, he might haue married her, or haue done what him listed")—the hero, who has almost single-handed defeated hundreds of warriors, receives a mysterious wound in the hour of his triumph and is removed from the scene. The following Ciceronian eulogy is thereupon pronounced:

What shall I say? but thus we lost him that, in all his proceedings, made Iustice his first guid, and experience his second; ever hating baseness, sloth, pride, and indignitie more then any dangers; that never allowed more for himselfe then his souldiers with him; that vpon no danger, would send them where he would not lead them himselfe; that would never see us want what he either had, or could by any meanes get vs; that would rather want then borrow, or starue then not pay; that loved actions more than wordes, and hated falshood and cousnage worse then death; whose adventures were our liues, and whose losse our deathes (I, 167).[9]

An epilogue of four pages narrates the coming of Sir Thomas Dale, and a final paragraph drives home the ethical lesson:

To conclude the historie, leauing this assurance to all posteritie, howe vnprosperously things may succeed, by what changes or chances soever; the action is honorable and worthie to bee approved, the defect whereof hath only beene in the managing the businesse (I, 173).

[9] The references are to the Arber-Bradley edition of Smith.

The most striking rhetorical feature of the *Proceedings* is undoubtedly the eighteen set speeches placed in the mouths of some of the chief actors, ten being given to Smith, five to Powhatan, and the rest to three other Indians. It is a fair guess that these were the work of the learned Dr. Simmonds, who might plead with Thucydides that

the speeches are given in the language in which, as it seemed to me, the several speakers would express, on the subjects under consideration, the sentiments most befitting the occasion.[10]

Classical example from Herodotus downward justified the writing of formal (if brief) orations in English for the great "king," Powhatan, who thrice pictures his own grandeur and who is made to deal with the invaders much in the spirit of Calgacus in the *Agricola.* The following stately discourse has a Roman ring:

Captaine *Smith,* you may vnderstand that I, hauing seene the death of all my people thrice, and not one living of those 3 generations but my selfe, I knowe the difference of peace and warre better then any in my Countrie. But now I am old, and ere long must die. My brethren, namely *Opichapam; Opechankanough,* and *Kekataugh,* my two sisters, and their two daughters are distinctly each others successours. I wish their experiences no less then mine and your loue to them, no lesse then mine to you: but this brute from *Nansamund,* that you are come to destroy my Countrie, so much affrighteth all my people, as they dare not visit you. What will it availe you to take that perforce, you may quietly haue with loue, or to destroy them that provide you food? What can you

---

[10] Thucydides, *History of the Peloponnesian War,* I, xxii (Loeb Library, 1919, trans. C. Foster Smith, I, 39).

get by war, when we can hide our provision and flie
to the woodes, whereby you must famish, by wrong-
ing vs your friends? And whie are you thus iealous of
our loues, seeing vs vnarmed, and both doe, and are
willing still to feed you with that you cannot get but
by our labours? Think you I am so simple not to
knowe it is better to eate good meate, lie well, and
sleepe quietly with my women and children, laugh
and be merrie with you, haue copper, hatchets, or
what I want, being your friend; then bee forced to
flie from al, to lie cold in the woods, feed vpon
acorns roots and such trash, and be so hunted by you
that I can neither rest eat nor sleepe, but my tired
men must watch, and if a twig but breake, everie one
crie, there comes Captaine *Smith:* then must I flie I
knowe not whether, and thus with miserable feare
end my miserable life, leauing my pleasures to such
youths as you, which, through your rash vnadvised-
nesse, may quickly as miserably ende, for want of
that you never knowe how to find? Let this therefore assure you of our loues, and everie yeare our
friendly trade shall furnish you with corne; and now
also if you would come in friendly manner to see vs,
and not thus with your gunnes and swords, as to in-
vade your foes (I, 135–36).[11]

This is obviously unhistorical and is certainly calculated to redound to the glory of Captain Smith, but
as writing it is firmly textured and beautifully built;
and in this paragraph, as in other speeches in this
work, the melancholy of a dying race has already appealed to the imagination of its conquerors. Smith, of
course, whether he is reproving the lazy, asserting
his authority, or defying Opechancanough to single
combat, is made to talk like the central figure of a

---

[11] Cf. in this connection the two orations in the *Agricola* of Tacitus:
that by Calgacus ("they make a solitude and call it peace") and that
by Agricola, cc. 30–34.

heroic play, and *sententiae* fall appropriately from his lips:

> Worse then is past cannot happen, and there is as much danger to returne, as to proceed forward.
> As for the dangers of our enemies, in such warres consist our chiefest pleasure.
> Remember it is fit for kings to keepe their promise.

Such language was never spoken by a wandering soldier of fortune and a guttural Indian, but a sense of mighty consequences hanging on these encounters makes such writing imaginatively proper.

But the *Proceedings* has more than formal structure; it has cogency. At Jamestown Smith's enemies are, to be sure, monotonously incompetent, and when Smith leaves they invariably lapse from virtue; but the tract really does give the effect that Smith like Caesar had to do all things at one time. Furthermore, real psychological insight is shown in the portraits of Smith and Powhatan, particularly when they confront each other for the last time. The book also exhibits considerable emotional range, including humor,[12] and has a certain moral dignity, as in the scene resembling a Jacobean play, when, after the drowning of Lieutenant Scrivener and eight others,

> To advertise the President [Smith] of this heavie newes, none could bee found would vndertake it: but the iourney was often refused of all in the fort, vntill *Master Wiffin* vndertooke alone the performance thereof. . . . This vnhappie newes, the President

[12] "We found . . . abundance of fish lying so thicke with their heads aboue the water, as for want of nets . . . we attempted to catch them with a frying pan; but we found it a bad instrument to catch fish with" (I, 113).

swore him to conceale from the rest; and so, dissembling his sorrow with the best countenance he could, when the night approached, went safely abord with all his companie (I, 144).

The work is capable of vivid description as in the incident of thirty naked Indian girls dancing in the wood (I, 123–24); of fresh figurative language, as in Ocanindge's speech:

If hee haue offended you in escaping your imprisonment, the fishes swim, the fowles flie, and the very beastes striue to escape the snare and liue: then blame not him being a man (I, 152);

and of that wordplay which satisfied the Jacobean quest for style, as in: "Yet what he carefully provided, the rest carelessly spent (I, 97)."

Other lesser writings, such as Lord de la Warr's *Relation* [13] (1611), Alexander Whitaker's *Good Newes from Virginia* (1613),[14] and John Rolfe's *Re-*

---

[13] Thomas West, Baron de la Warr (1577–1618), appointed first governor and captain-general of Virginia, brought 150 emigrants to Jamestown June 10, 1610, and so saved the colony from dispersal. He returned to England in June, 1611, and printed his *Relation,* which may have been penned by William Strachey. He died on a second voyage to the New World June 7, 1618. See the account by A. F. Pollard in *DNB* and that by Isabel M. Calder in *DAB.*

The Relation of the Right Honourable the Lord De-La-Warre, Lord Gouernour and Captaine Generall of the Colonie, planted in Virginea was published as a small quarto in London in 1611 by "authority" of the Council for Virginia and immediately reprinted. A facsimile edition of 50 copies was published in London in 1858 by C. Whittingham, and an edition of 20 copies in facsimile by the Heliotype Company was published in New York in 1867 (?). Purchas included the *Relation* in *Pvrchas His Pilgrimes* (IV, 1762–1764; in the MacLehose edition, XIX, 85–90). The work is also available in Tyler's *Narratives of Early Virginia,* pp. 207–214.

[14] Son of William Whitaker, master of St. John's College and Regius Professor of Divinity at Cambridge, Alexander Whitaker was born in 1585; received his B.A. from Cambridge in 1604/5, his M.A. in 1608; and upon ordination served in the north of England until

lation of the State of Virginia (?1616) [15] belong
rather to "promotion" literature than to that of the

he volunteered to go to Jamestown with the expedition of Sir Thomas
Dale in 1611. He ministered to Henricopolis and Bermuda Hundred,
fifty miles up the James, and was drowned in 1617.

Good Newes from Virginia, prefaced by a dedicatory epistle from
William Crashawe to Lord Ure, was published in London in 1613;
partially reprinted in *Pvrchas His Pilgrimes* (ed. cit., XIX, 110–116)
and republished in facsimile in the Scholars' Facsimiles & Reprints
series (New York, 1936). A letter to Crashawe (1611) to be found
in Brown, *Genesis of the United States,* I, 497–500; one to Sir
Thomas Smyth (1612), *ibid.,* II, 578–579; and one to the Rev. William Gouge (1614) in E. L. Godwin, *The Colonial Church in Virginia* (Milwaukee and London, 1927), pp. 41–42, constitute his literary remains. Only a small portion of the *Good Newes from Virginia,*
which is in sermon form, is a transcript of Whitaker's observation.
This work should be distinguished from a rare broadside ballad
bearing the same title, for the text of which see *William and Mary
Quarterly,* 3d ser., V (1948), 351–358.

[15] Son of John and Dorothea Mason Rolfe, John Rolfe was baptized
May 6, 1585, at Heacham in Norfolk. He married in 1608; sailed
with his wife for Virginia in June, 1609; and was wrecked on the
Bermudas, where a daughter was born and died. Upon their arrival
in Jamestown his wife also died. In 1612 Rolfe succeeded in produc-
ing a commercially profitable tobacco; in April, 1614, he married
Pocahontas; in 1616 he and his wife returned to England, where the
Indian "princess" died and where Rolfe wrote his *Relation.* He returned to Virginia in May, 1617; in 1621, having been secretary and
recorder of the colony, he became a member of the council; he married a third time; and he was killed in the massacre of 1622. See the
accounts by Thomas Seccombe in *DNB* and by T. J. Wertenbaker in
DAB.

Rolfe's *Relation,* which is in the form of a letter to the king, was
published in the *Southern Literary Messenger,* V (1839), 401–406,
under the heading: "Interesting Account of Virginia, In 1617." For
Rolfe's most important letter see below, p. 34.

Rolfe's observations on the government of the colony still preserve
their interest. The greatest need of all, he said, "is good and sufficient men, as well of birth and qualitie, to command soldiers" as well
as good workmen. For two years the colony "was governed by a
president and councell, aristocratically," "in which tyme such envie,
dissentions and jarres were daily sowne" as almost to wreck the enterprise, but when "a more absolute government was graunted, mo-
narchially," improvement eventually set in.

colony, and the reports of Captain Samuel Argall, though invaluable to the historian, do not differ greatly in substance or style from those of his compeers.[16] There is, however, so much firsthand observation of American Life in Ralph Hamor's *Trve Discovrse* (1615) [17] as to throw it definitely into the category of American writing. Unfortunately for the American muse, Hamor's pamphlet is badly organized, badly written, and badly printed. The title page evidences the confusion of Hamor's aim: "A Trve

[16] Aside from the fact that he was descended from a Kentish family, nothing is known of Sir Samuel Argall until 1609. He explored a shorter route to the New World in that year; sailed again with the de la Warr expedition of 1610; and included among his accomplishments a voyage to Cape Cod from Jamestown, the kidnapping of Pocahontas, the breaking up of French settlements in Maine (1613), and service in Virginia as deputy governor (1617). He afterwards served in the Mediterranean, dying about 1641. See the account by C. H. Coote in *DNB* and that by P. A. Bruce in *DAB*. Characteristic accounts of his actions may be read in Purchas, *ed. cit.,* XIX, 73–84, 90–95.

[17] Ralph Hamor (birth date unknown) was the son of Ralph Hamor the elder, a merchant tailor of London and a member (like his son) of the Virginia Company. The younger Hamor came to Jamestown in 1609 and remained until 1614, publishing in 1615 his *Trve Discovrse.* He returned from England to Jamestown in May, 1618, and was appointed a member of the council. In 1622 he successfully defended his home against the Indians. He seems to have been an Indian trader; he married a widow, Mrs. Elizabeth Clements; and from 1611 to 1614 he served as recorder for the colony. He died some time after March 22, 1627/28. The best biographical sketch is that in Lyon Gardiner Tyler, *Encyclopedia of Virginia Biography* (New York, 1915), I, 81–82.

A Trve Discovrse of the Present Estate of Virginia, and the successe of the affaires there till the 18 of Iune. 1614 . . . Written by Raphe Hamor the yonger, late Secretarie in that Colony was printed in London in 1615. An edition of 200 copies in type facsimile was published in Albany in 1860. Most of Hamor is included in *Purchas His Pilgrimes* (*ed. cit.,* XIX, 95–102). Citations in the text are from the Albany reprint.

Discovrse of the Present Estate of Virginia, and the successe of the affaires there till the 18 of Iune. 1614. Together. With a Relation of the seuerall English Townes and fortes, the assured hopes of that countrie and the peace concluded with the Indians. The Christening of Powhatans daughter and her marriage with an Englishman." A talent for organization might have created unity out of this hodgepodge, but organization is precisely the quality Hamor does not have. Verbal awkwardness almost, but not quite, spoils even entertaining material, including a comic scene in which Hamor and Thomas Savage appear as emissaries at the "court" of Powhatan to ask a daughter of that "emperor" in "marriage" with Sir Thomas Dale, who had a wife in England. Here Hamor's loquacity is an asset, for he puts everything down—Powhatan's greeting of an English boy, the savage's hearty laughter at hearing of Pocahontas's happiness, the oyster shells which are made into bead money, the bread (which "was brought in two great wodden bouls, the quantity of a bushel sod breade made vp round, of the bignesse of a tenise ball") and the fleas, which drove them out of an Indian hut to a mat "under a broade oake." These are valid touches, but as a whole Hamor's *Discovrse* is poor stuff.

Three letters are appended to it, one of which will always retain its human interest. This is from John Rolfe to Sir Thomas Dale,[18] and relates the turmoils of spirit through which that widower progressed to his wedding with a bride "whose education hath bin

[18] In more accurate form the letter may be read in *Virginia Magazine of History and Biography,* XXII (1914), 152–157 and also in Tyler's *Narratives of Early Virginia,* pp. 239–244. The quotations in the text are, however, from the Hamor version.

rude, her manners barbarous, her generation accursed." Inasmuch as this letter is enclosed in one from the Rev. Alexander Whitaker to a London friend, it is scarcely a private communication; yet those who look upon Pilgrim and Puritan as peculiarly introspective may ponder this revelation of more secular psychology:

Thus when I had thought I had obtained my peace and quietnesse, beholde another, but more gracious tentation hath made breaches into my holiest and strongest meditations; with which I haue bin put to a new triall, in a straighter manner then the former: for besides the many passions and sufferings vvhich I haue daily, hourely, yea and in my sleepe indured, euen awaking mee to astonishment, taxing mee with remisnesse, and carelesnesse, refusing and neglecting to performe the duteie of a good Christian, pulling me by the eare, and crying: why dost not thou indeuour to make her a Christian? And these haue happened to my greater wonder, euen when she hath bin furthest seperated from me, which is common reason (were it not an vndoubted worke of God) might breede forgetfulnesse of a farre more worthie creature. Besides, I say the holy spirit of God hath often demaunded of me, why I was created? If not for transitory pleasures and worldly vanities, but to labour in the Lords vineyard, there to sow and plant, to nourish and increase the fruites thereof, daily adding with the good husband in the Gospell, somewhat to the tallent, that in the end the fruites may be reaped, to the comfort of the laborer in this life, and his saluation in the world to come?

Rolfe wrestles with love, divinity, and politics through eight pages of text.

3. THE LITERATURE OF EXPLORATION AND SETTLEMENT: THE MAJOR WRITERS

SUCH WERE WHAT MAY BE TERMED THE MINOR WRITERS OF THE FIRST GENERATION. THE MAJOR AUTHORS OF THE SAME GENERATION WERE CAPTAIN JOHN SMITH, William Strachey, and John Pory; and if Smith[1] is the best known of this trio, with no desire to be startling, it may be said of his celebrity that it is due in greater

[1] Son of George and Alice Smith, John Smith was born in Willoughby, Lincolnshire, being baptized January 9, 1579/80. After a grammar school education, he was apprenticed to a merchant; but not liking that life, he became a soldier of fortune who fought against the Turks, by whom he was captured and sold into slavery, if his story is to be believed. He escaped and returned to England in 1604. In 1606 he sailed with the Jamestown colonists, and in 1607 he was made a member of the governing council in Virginia. His work there as an explorer, soldier, ruler, and purveyor of supplies is too well known to require summary. In 1608-9 he became president of the council; in October, 1609, partly because of injuries resulting from a powder explosion (see above, pp. 15–17), he returned to England. In 1608 was published *A Trve Relation of such occurrences and accidents of noate as hath hapned in Virginia since the first planting of that Collony,* which in its third "state" is attributed on the title page to Smith. In 1612 his *A Map of Virginia* was printed at Oxford, the first of the so-called Oxford tracts (see above, pp. 25–30). In 1616 Smith published *A Description of New England;* in 1620, *New*

degree to his deeds and his personality than to his
achievement in literature. The story of his rescue by
Pocahontas, which has become a part of American

Englands Trials (second edition, with altered text, 1622). In 1624
appeared *The Generall Historie of Virginia, New-England, and the
Summer Isles,* compiled by Smith and partly written by him. *An Accidence or The Path-way to Experience* (also known as *An Accidence
for Young Sea-men* and as *The Seaman's Grammar,* 1627) was first
published in 1626 and evinces a passion for the navy which led
Smith, before he died, to contemplate writing a history of the sea. In
1614 he had explored the New England coast and been captured and
detained by pirates, but *The True Travels, Adventvres, and Observations of Captaine Iohn Smith,* 1630, does not come down that
far, although it extends in time beyond the *Generall Historie.* His
last publication was his *Advertisements For the unexperienced
Planters of New-England, or anywhere,* 1631. Little is known of his
later years. In the *History of the Worthies of England* Fuller, who
got his information from one of Smith's relatives, says that Smith
"led his old age in London, where his having a prince's mind imprisoned in a poor man's purse rendered him to the contempt of such
who were not ingenuous" (ed. pub. in London, 1840, I, 276). Smith
died June 21, 1631.

Recent discoveries about Smith's earlier years have not only
severely shaken the common charge that he is untrustworthy as the
chronicler of his own adventures but have also antiquated most of
the earlier biographies. On Smith's career in Hungary, Transylvania,
and so on, see Laura Polanyi Striker's translation from the German
of J. Franz Pichler, "Captain John Smith in the Light of Styrian
Sources," *Virginia Magazine of History and Biography,* LXV
(1957), 332–354; her "The Hungarian Historian, Lewis L. Kropf,
on Captain John Smith's *True Travels,*" *ibid.,* LXVI (1958), 23–43,
and Philip L. Barbour, "Captain John Smith's Observations on Life
in Tartary," *ibid.,* LXVIII (1960), 271–283. See also *The Life of
John Smith, English Soldier by Henry Wharton,* translated from the
Latin Manuscript with an Essay on Captain John Smith in Seventeenth-Century Literature by Laura Polanyi Striker, published for
the Virginia Historical Society by the University of North Carolina
Press (Chapel Hill, 1957; now distributed by the University Press of
Virginia, Charlottesville). Biographies which deal with this new
material are Bradford Smith, *Captain John Smith* (New York, 1953),
and Philip L. Barbour, *The Three Worlds of Captain John Smith*
(Boston, 1964). The best bibliography of Smith is still Wilberforce
Eames, *A Bibliography of Captain John Smith* (New York, 1927),

folklore, he did not print until he was forty-four, when the "Nomparell" of Virginia had been seven years dead and Smith had not seen America for ten years, nor Virginia for fifteen. This famous episode occupies part of a paragraph in the *Generall Historie,* a folio of 248 pages, many of them not by Smith, and the disproportion between legend and origin is of symbolic significance. Most of the controversy concerning the captain has revolved about his work as an administrator and his credibility as a witness; critical attention has scarcely been directed to the writer who spent the last twenty years of his life as a propagandist for the colonial idea. "You may see plainely," he wrote in 1622,

the yearely successe from *New England* (by *Virginia*) which has bin so costly to this kingdome and so deare to me, which either to see perish or but bleed, pardon me though it passionate me beyond the bounds of modestie, to haue bin sufficiently able to foresee it, and had neither power nor meanes how to preuent it. By that acquaintance I haue with them, I may call them my children; for they haue bin my wife, my hawks, my hounds, my cards, my dice, and in totall my best content, as indifferent to my heart as my left hand to my right.[2]

reprinted from Sabin's *Dictionary.* The standard edition is the *Travels and Works of Captain John Smith,* ed. Edward Arber, new edition with a biographical and critical introduction by A. G. Bradley, 2 parts (i.e., volumes) (Edinburgh, 1910), recently reprinted.

Somewhat remote in its bearing on Smith is *A True Relation of the State of Virginia Lefte by Sir Thomas Dale Knight in May Last 1616.* By John Rolfe (New Haven, 1951). The eighteen pages of the original manuscript (written in England) are reproduced in facsimile, and the introduction and notes are by a group of Virginia librarians. The introduction presents Rolfe as a man of "peace" in contradistinction to more warlike Virginians.

[2] "New Englands Trials," 2d ed., 1622, *Travels and Works,* I, 265.

This is movingly said, but it is Smith's achievement as a writer rather than as an executor with which one is here concerned.

Of the author, in an interpretative chapter of singular charm and insight, Charles Dudley Warner observed over half a century ago that

> as a writer he was wholly untrained, but with all his introversions and obscurities he is the most readable chronicler of his time, the most amusing and as untrustworthy as any. He is influenced by his prejudices, though not so much by them as by his imagination and vanity. He had a habit of accurate observation, as his maps show, and this trait gives to his statements and descriptions, when his own reputation is not concerned, a value beyond that of those of most contemporary travelers.[3]

It is questionable, however, whether any amount of literary "training" would have altered the writing habits of one who swaggers like Captain Dalgetty and who "faintly suggests a moral Falstaff," in Warner's illuminating phrase. It must be remembered how little of what the captain wrote comes to us from his original manuscript. Either his own composition was altered for the worse by others, as in his first pamphlet, or he himself so jumbled together original material and the reports of others as to bewilder the unhistorical reader. Moreover, Smith (like Cotton Mather) persisted in emptying an earlier work into a later one; and though the old wine may not burst the new bottle, the elements of the new brew

---

[3] *Captain John Smith* (Lives of American Worthies; New York, 1881), p. 303. But Warner could not escape his age: "Another thing [is] to be said about his [Smith's] writings. They are uncommonly clean for his day. Only here and there is coarseness encountered." The modern reader looks for this "coarseness" vainly.

do not perfectly mix. One might suppose, if only in the interest of his amusing egotism, Smith would have sought clarity of style, but this curious repetitive practice results in prose that is sometimes clumsy and unintelligible—pronouns lose their referents, syntax collapses, the sequence of ideas vanishes in a succession of hasty clauses, and the exhausted sentence sinks into a morass of vocables. But the reader must not falter. The next page is likely to yield vivid description, swift narrative, dramatic character work, and a compact and trenchant style. It is notable that *An Accidence* and *Advertisements For the unexperienced Planters,* which come closest to achieving unity of tone and structure, are customarily passed over in favor of these huge, sprawling, many-faceted, but always racy compilations, the *Generall Historie* and the *True Travels.* How much of his unskillfulness is due to haste, how much to the intrusion of other styles from narratives copied into Smith's own text it is now difficult to say, but the disharmony is characteristic. Vain, mercurial, self-seeking, yet devoted to a cause; dogged and irresponsible; half genius and half charlatan, the only secular Elizabethan in American literature is, by a wild paradox, incarnate proof of the dictum that the style *is* the man.

Important as was Smith's contribution to the preservation of Jamestown, his American adventures were but the last of a strange, eventful history which stretched, if he is to be believed, from Russia to Ireland and from the condition of a Turkish slave to the presidency of Virginia. His travels had taught him the importance of sea power;[4] and it is signifi-

---

[4] "Then you might build ships of any proportion and numbers you please, fiue times cheaper then you can doe here, and haue good

cant that after his return from Jamestown there are
traces of his familiar intercourse with Purchas, the
heir of Hakluyt, and of his reading of Dr. John Dee.
Such fragments of Smith's correspondence as have
been printed were directed to the philosophic chan-
cellor at a time when Bacon was meditating the theory of colonization. No less a person than Dr. William Simmonds took pains to put together the second
part of *A Map of Virginia,* and no less a dignitary
than Sir Robert Cotton (author of a *Memorial on
Abuses of the Navy,* 1608) urged Smith to write his
autobiography.[5] The *Generall Historie* was published
at the desire of the Virginia Company, *An Accidence*
was "caused to bee printed by my worthy friend, Sir
Samuel Saltonstall," the *True Travels* was dedicated
to the Earls of Pembroke, Lindsey, and Dover. These
facts have long been known, but in their eagerness to
dramatize Smith as a mere soldier of fortune historians have sometimes failed to perceive that in England he moved in excellent intellectual company. He
was one of a group of imperialists and contributed to

---

merchandize for their fraught in this vnknowne Land, to the aduance-
ment of Gods glory, his Church and Gospel; and the strengthning
and releefe of a great part of Christendome without hurt to any; to
the terror of Pirats, the amazement of enemies, the assistance of
friends, the securing Merchants, and so much increase of Nauigation,
to make *Englands* trade and shipping as much as any Nations in the
world: besides a hundred other benefits, to the generall good of all
true subiects, and would cause thousands yet vnborne to blesse the
time, and all them that first put it in practise" ("Generall Historie,"
Travels and Works, II, 775; cf. I, 247, 271).

[5] Characteristic of Smith's independence is the fact that the *True
Travels,* with its defiant statement that "Sir *Robert Cotton,* that most
learned Treasurer of Antiquitie," whose "noble desire I could not but
in part satisfie," was his friend and that the work was entered for
publication in 1629, the very year that Cotton was arrested and imprisoned by the king's order. See *Travels and Works,* II, 808.

the great debate over the empire. He brought to the discussion immediate experience in an English colony and a cosmopolitan point of view,[6] so that there is justice in the observation of Jarvis M. Morse that

the historical writings of Captain John Smith were conceived in an expansive spirit, for the purpose of presenting a broad view of British achievements in the western hemisphere. Smith undertook for America what Hakluyt and Purchas had projected for the world at large, the compilation of a complete account of exploration and colonial settlement. It was a noble ambition, under the quickening influence of which he wrote untiringly to the year of his death.[7]

Hakluyt was both a skillful editor and a modest man, whereas Smith was clumsy in the one capacity and boastful in the other. Nevertheless, Morse touches the central theme of Smith's work, however sprawling and disorganized that work may seem. His twelve publications fit with unexpected coherence into a single plan. The *True Travels* pictures the practical education of the future frontiersman and colonial commander; the historical works both record events and moralize upon them; and *An Accidence* and the *Advertisements For the unexperienced Planters* outline

---

[6] Note the opening of "Advertisements For the unexperienced Planters:" "The Warres in *Europe, Asia,* and *Affrica,* taught me how to subdue the wilde Salvages in *Virginia* and *New-England* in *America,*" so that after much ignorant controversy it has "pleased God now at last to stirre up some good mindes, that I hope will produce glory to God, honour to his Majesty, and profit to his Kingdomes" (*Travels and Works,* II, 925–926).

[7] "John Smith and His Critics: A Chapter in Colonial Historiography," *Journal of Southern History,* I (1935), 123. This is the most compact summary of scholarship about Smith available at that date. "America" in the quotation must of course include Bermuda, in view of the fifth book of the *Generall Historie.*

a general practical education for mariners who were to carry Englishmen abroad and for settlers who were to hold plantations against the nation's enemies.

The first account of the Jamestown settlement to appear in print, the *Trve Relation,* has an air of having been hurriedly written up from notes in order to be dispatched to England (in the summer of 1607); but how Smith's manuscript fell into the hands of the "I. H." who signs the verbose preface, why it was at one time thought to be by Thomas Watson, and whether, in addition to suppressing parts of Smith's original manuscript, the "editor" also included matter not by Smith [8] are questions which have never been settled. Haste in writing, haste in "editing," and haste in printing do all they can to mar this work, which is nevertheless in particular moments vivid and

[8] It is difficult to believe that the man who wrote as directly as this: "As yet we had no houses to couer vs, our Tents were rotten, and our Cabbins worse then nought: our best commodities was Yron which we made into little chissels" (*Travels and Works,* I, 9), also wrote the verbose concluding sentence: "Wee now remaining being in good health, all our men wel contented, free from mutinies, in loue one with another, and as we hope in a continuall peace with the Indians: where we doubt not but by Gods gracious assistance, and the aduenturers willing minds and speedie furtherance to so honorable an action, in after times to see our Nation to enioy a Country, not onely exceeding pleasant for habitation, but also very profitable for comerce in generall; no doubt pleasing to almightie God, honourable to our gracious Soueraigne, and commodious generally to the whole Kingdome" (I, 40).

This unctuousness is contradicted by the pamphlet itself and by Smith's subsequent accounts both of factions in the settlement and of the treachery of the Indians. One inclines to agree with Charles Poindexter (*Captain John Smith and His Critics* [Richmond, 1893], p. 41), albeit on other grounds than his, that Smith's letter was "perverted and distorted by this editor, J. H., for a purpose of which we may fairly conjecture"—i.e., stockjobbing in the interests of the Virginia Company. The *Trve Relation* plays an unexpectedly small part in the make-up of the *Generall Historie.*

dramatic. The seizure of Smith by Opechancanough's
Indians is tellingly written, and the descriptions of
Indian life, conditioned though these are by Smith's
persistent reading of a feudal order into their society,
are as absorbing now as then:

Approaching their Towne, which was within 6
miles where I was taken, onely made as arbors and
couered with mats, which they remoue as occasion requires: all the women and children, being aduertised
of this accident, came foorth to meet them, the
King well guarded with 20 bowmen 5 flanck and rear,
and each flanck before him a sword and a peece, and
after him the like, then a bowman, then I on each
hand a boweman, the rest in file in the reare, which
reare led foorth amongst the trees in a bishion [*sic*],
eache his bowe and a handfull of arrowes, a quiuer
at his back grimly painted: on eache flanck a sargeant,
the one running alwaies towards the front, the other
towards the reare, each a true pace and in exceeding good order (I, 16).

This, to be sure, is a little like the triumphant pro-
cession which concludes *Peter and the Wolf,* but
Smith's first interview with Powhatan is admirable
word painting; his reporting of the ceremonies by
which the medicine men hoped to steal the stranger's
magic, and the second interview with the "emperor,"
in which Smith records their dialogue, exhibit his
practical eye for detail and his memory for organization:

Two in a ranke we marched to the Emperors
house. Before his house stood fortie or fiftie great
Platters of fine bread. Being entred the house, with
loude tunes they all made signes of great ioy. This
proude saluage, hauing his finest women, and the
principall of his chiefe men assembled, sate in rankes

as before is expressed : himself as vpon a Throne at the vpper ende of the house, with such a Maiestie as I cannot expresse, nor yet haue often seene, either in Pagan or Christian. With a kinde countenance hee bad mee welcome, and caused a place to bee made by himselfe [for me] to sit.

I presented him a sute of red cloath, a white Greyhound, and a Hatte: as Iewels he esteemed them, and with a great Oration made by three of his Nobles, if there be any amongst Saluages, kindly accepted them, with a publike confirmation of a perpetuall league and friendship (I, 24–25).

The conversation which follows shows Indians heartily laughing at a joke, and the lie with which it concludes reveals the hollowness of the hope for a "perpetuall league and friendship." The supposition that Smith hastily threw this manuscript together is increased by the unconscious revelation of his own fears and perplexities,[9] since in subsequent accounts of his conduct he represents himself as being on all occasions farsighted and firm. It is also significant that the proportion of general comment and exhortation in the *Trve Relation* is small, whereas the propagandistic nature of Smith's later writings leads him into endless hortatory intrusions upon the narrative.

Inasmuch as Smith's other historical pamphlets were gathered (save for the *True Travels*) into the *Generall Historie,* one may next turn to two minor works not thus compounded. Whatever its value as a practical handbook for apprentice mariners, *An Accidence* is distinguished by succinctness of phrase and colloquialism of diction. Perhaps the first printed

[9] See the shrewd analysis by John Gould Fletcher, *John Smith— Also Pocahontas* (New York, 1928), chaps. vii ff.

book in English on seamanship and naval terminology
(the claim is disputed), it reads at times like the
opening scene of *The Tempest:*

> We are shot through and through, and betweene
> winde and water, trye the pumpe. Maister let vs
> breathe and refreshe a little. Sling a man ouerboord
> to stop the leake. Done, done. Is all ready againe,
> Yea, yea: beare vp close with him, with all your great
> and small shot charge him. Boord him on his weather
> quarter, lash fast your graplins and sheare off, then
> run stemlins the mid ships. Boord and boord, or
> thwart the hawse, we are foule on each other.
> The ships on fire. Cut any thing to get cleere, and
> smother the fire with wet clothes. We are cleere, and
> the fire is out, God be thanked (II, 796–797).

Unfortunately for Smith's reputation, this lively
work now needs a glossary to interpret it. The same
necessity, however, does not obtain in the case of the
*Advertisements For the unexperienced Planters of
New-England, or any where,* a pamphlet of some 48
pages, dedicated to the Archbishops of Canterbury
and York. "Malignancy, I expect," he informs the
reader, especially from those that "can neither shift
Sun nor Moone, nor say their Compasse, yet will
tell you of more than all the world, betwixt the *Exchange, Pauls* and *Westminster";* and this note of
sardonic humor everywhere informs a work which is
less a handbook of advice for John Winthrop's colony than a crotchety *apologia pro vita sua* in which
Smith takes leave of a world which had vexed him
into a disillusioned tolerance of fools. The London
Company seemed to "thinke all the world was Oatmeale" in Virginia, where gentlemen went on build-
ing forts when "an Egge shell" would have sufficed.
What could one expect of gentlemanly futility? As

well attempt to "hew Rocks with Oister-shels" he says of idlers who seemed to think that in America "houses and all those commodities did grow naturally"; and his contemptuous description of the setting out of Lord de la Warr is a gem of humorous disparagement:

At least [they] got a Commission in their owne names, promising the King custome within seven yeares, where we were free for one and twenty; appointing the Lord *De-la-ware* for Governour, with as many great and stately officers, and offices under him, as doth belong to a great Kingdome, with good summes for their extraordinary expences; also privileges for Cities; Charters for Corporations, Universities, Free-scholes, and Glebe-land; putting all those in practice before there was either people, students, or schollers to build or use them, or provision or victuall to feed them were then there (II, 929).

He had only contempt for the discontented.[10] To be sure, "all that returned are not of those humors" and Winthrop was a "noble Governour," but the human race generally is characterized by the stupidity that leads "tender educats" to New England, transports others to Virginie to "doe nothing but complaine, curse, and despaire," sends out ships with false maps and unskillful pilots, insists on too much paper work, and surrounds an empire builder like John Smith with

[10] "Some two hundred of the rest he [Winthrop] was content to returne for *England,* whose clamors are as variable as their humours and Auditors. Some say they could see no timber of two feet diameter, some the Country is all Woods; others they drunke all the Springs and Ponds dry, yet like to famish for want of fresh water; some of the danger of the rattell Snake; and that others sold their provisions at what rates they pleased to them that wanted, and so returned to *England* great gainers out of other miseries" (II, 954–955).

a "trecherous company that betrayed me," though he labor like Hercules from the most disinterested motives. His only recompense was slander and some barren rocks called *"Smiths* Isles," "the most overgrowne with such shrubs and sharpe whins you can hardly passe them; without either grasse or wood but three or foure short shrubby old Cedars." If only colonists were led by competent gentlemen, kept in order by good laws and an established church, and freed of the vices of communism!

It is time, however, to turn to Smith's larger works. The *Generall Historie,* projected as early as April, 1621, published in 1624, exhibits signs of haste, for which the author apologizes no further than to excuse the "stile of a Souldier." No part of the material was prepared *ab origine* for this compilation. Books II and VI are, as Smith would say, "writ with his owne hand": that is, they are revised and augmented versions of *A Map of Virginia* (1612), *A Description of New England* (1616), and *New Englands Trials* (1620; 1622). Book I, in which Smith traces the history of British North America downward from Madoc, Prince of Wales, is put together out of Hakluyt and other sources; Book III is a reprint (with augumentations) of *The Proceedings of the English Colonie in Virginia* (1612); Book IV is built of *miscellanea;* and Book V, the history of the "Summer Iles," was taken out of a manuscript written by an English official in Bermuda. In putting this material together Smith is not always careful: now and then he alters figures arbitrarily; he refers to himself sometimes in the first person, sometimes in the third; and he is not careful to distinguish among persons using "I." Confusion in the printing house occasions the presence of a sheaf of complimentary verses in the midst of the prose. Nevertheless, working under pressure, the author does his best to correct his originals in the light of the most recent information and strives after edification by the interpolation of *sententiae* in prose and verse, the verse almost uniformly bad.

Books II and III are the parts by which Smith is best remembered. The *Map of Virginia,* whether in its original or in its revised form, is one of the best accounts of Indian culture in Virginia which have come down to us and in both style and organization shows how excellent an observer Smith could be, how trenchantly he wrote when his personal repute was not involved. Other explorers give us an equivalent amount of anthropological lore; Smith dramatizes. His capacity to make description march is well illustrated in such passages as these:

One Salvage hunting alone, vseth the skinne of a Deere slit on the one side, and so put on his arme, through the neck, so that his hand comes to the head which is stuffed, and the hornes, head, eyes, eares, and every part as artificially counterfeited as they can devise. Thus shrowding his body in the skinne by stalking, he approacheth the Deere, creeping on the ground from one tree to another. If the Deere chance to find fault, or stand at gaze, he turneth the head with his hand to his best advantage to seeme like a Deere, also gazing and licking himselfe. So watching his best advantage to approach, having shot him, he chaseth him by his bloud and straine till he get him.

Fifteen of the properest young boyes, betweene ten and fifteene yeares of age they painted white. Having brought them forth, the people spent the forenoone in dancing and singing about them with Rattles.

In the afternoone they put those children to the roote of a tree. By them all the men stood in a guard, every one having a Bastinado in his hand, made of reeds bound together. This made a lane be-tweene them all along, through which there were ap-pointed fiue young men to fetch these children: so every one of the fiue went through the guard to fetch a childe each after other by turnes, the guard fiercely beating them with their Bastinadoes, and they patiently enduring and receiuing all defending the children with their naked bodies from the vn-merciful blowes, that pay them soundly, though the children escape. All this while the women weepe and cry out very passionately, prouiding mats, skins, mosse, and dry wood, as things fitting their childrens funerals (I, 366, 373-374).

Of course Smith did not comprehend this ceremony, but his devouring eye has missed nothing, his "rude military hand" creates a picture as colorful as the paintings of Catlin.

Pocahontas moves in and out the second and third books of the *Generall Historie* with fawnlike grace; and though Smith, in reprinting his materials, introduced her at imaginative intervals in the *His-torie* where she did not appear in the earlier pam-phlets, the general reader is content to waive the question of authenticity in favor of imaginative truth.[11] She serves as an artistic foil to the doughty captain who, touching up his material, pictures him-self in the role of Julius Caesar doing everything at

[11] In Book IV (II, 530-534) Smith tells of meeting Pocahontas in England and of her dubious reception of a man who, in some sense, deceived her: "You did promise *Powhatan* what was yours should bee his, and he the like to you; you called him father being in his land a stranger, and by the same reason so must I doe you." On this whole episode see Fletcher, *op. cit.,* 282-284.

one time. It is not quite true that the alterations invariably add to the glory of the captain, yet there is something so engaging in the aplomb with which Smith edits his own actions and orations with an eye to posterity that one forgives him much. Certainly his worst enemy must be grateful for the "Copy of a Letter sent to the Treasurer and Councell of *Virginia* from Captaine *Smith,* then President in VIRGINIA," in which an exasperated administrator pays his respects to people at home who invent paper work. "Though I be no scholer," he says roundly, "I am past a schoole-boy; and I desire but to know, what either you, and these here, doe know but that I haue learned to tell you by the continuall hazard of my life." There is something wildly comic in his irritation at Newport's instructions to move a heavy boat into the upper reaches of the James: "If he had burnt her to ashes one might haue carried her in a bag; but as she is fiue hundred cannot, to a navigable place aboue the Falles." Smith minces no words: the coronation of Powhatan "will be the confusion of vs all"; "from your Ship we had not provision in victuals worth twenty pound"; Ratcliffe has changed his name to Sicklemore, "a poore counterfeited Imposture," and is being sent home "least the company should cut his throat"; and if more men are to come out, let them be "Carpenters, husbandmen, gardiners, fisher men, blacksmiths, masons, and diggers vp of trees." The letter ends: "These are the causes that haue kept vs in *Virginia,* from laying such a foundation, that ere this might haue given much better content and satisfaction; but as yet you must not looke for any profitable returns: so I humbly rest" (II, 442–445).

Book VI, or the New England [12] section of the *Generall Historie,* lacks the human interest of the Virginia books, inasmuch as the originals are expository propaganda pamphlets. In this section, however, Smith displays an unusual command of the economics of trade, labors the advantages of a navy, and writes persuasively on colony making. A survey of the fall of other kingdoms—for example, Rome and Constantinople—leads him to somber reflections upon wealth as a breeder of idleness and self-regard, in opposition to which he sets up a high ethical ideal of leading the English to "abound in honor, by Heroicall deeds of action, iudgement, pietie, and vertue. What was it both in their purse and person they would not doe, for the good of their Common-wealth, which might moue them presently to set out their spare children in these generous designes (II, 730). His conclusion to the *Description of New England* is noble prose:

Then seeing we are not borne for our selues, but each to help other, and our abilities are much alike at the houre of our birth, and the minute of our death: seeing our good deeds or our bad by faith in Christs merits, is all we haue, to carie our soules to heauen or hell. Seeing honor is our liues ambition, and our ambition after death to haue an honorable memory of our life: and seeing by no meanes we should be abated of the dignities and glories of our predecessors, let vs imitate their vertues to be worthily their successors.[13]

[12] As the Arber-Bradley edition points out, in reprinting the two New England pamphlets Smith added extracts from Dr. John Dee, *Mourt's Relation,* Edward Winslow, and Richard Whitbourne.

[13] So ends the original pamphlet; in the *Generall Historie* there is appended a tag from Lucretius, vilely translated and rhymed (II, 742).

Smith, however, weakens this grandeur by appeals to the self-interest of various classes of Englishmen, obscures the clear line of his narrative by flings at the malice and rascality of others,[14] and mixes the dry details of the fishing trade into excellent, if intermittent, descriptions of the New England coast.

The sixth book is also notable for containing Smith's ripest views on the nature of the state, retained verbatim from the two original pamphlets. He anticipates Adam Smith in supposing that men are led as by an invisible hand to labor for the social good:

> For necessity doth in these cases so rule a Commonwealth, and each in their seuerall functions, as their labours in their qualities may be as profitable, because there is a necessary mutuall vse of all (I, 213; II, 727).

The basis of the state is self-interest:

> For, I am not so simple to thinke, that euer any other motiue then wealth, will euer erect there a Commonweale; or draw companie from their ease and humours at home, to stay in *New England* to effect my purposes (I, 212; II, 726).

But though he believes in *laissez faire,* he is no democrat:

[14] Typical is the passage on "The trechery of Master *Hunt*": "But one *Thomas Hunt* the Master of this ship (when I was gone) thinking to preuent that intent I had to make there a Plantation, thereby to keepe this abounding Countrey still in obscuritie, that onely he and some few Merchants more might enioy wholly the benefit of the Trade, and profit of this Countrey, betraied foure and twenty of those poore Saluages aboord his ship: and most dishonestly, and inhumanely, for their kinde vsage of me and all our men, caried them with him to *Maligo,* and there for a little priuate gaine sold those silly Saluages for Rials of eight" (II, 698–699). Remembering Smith's lies to Powhatan, one remains unconvinced by this outburst of humanitarianism.

A

True relation of ſuch occurrences
and accidents of note,as hath hapned in *Vir-*
*ginia,*ſince the firſt planting of that Collony,
which is now reſident in the South part
thereof,till the laſt returne.

Inde Sir , commendations re-
membꝛed, &c. You ſhall vnderſtand
that after many croſſes in the downes
by tempeſts,wee arriued ſafely vppon
the Southweſt part of the great Ca-
naries:within foure oꝛ fiue daies after
we ſet ſaile foꝛ Dominica, the 26. of
Apꝛill: the firſt land we made,wee fell
with Cape Henry,the verie mouth of
the Bay of Chiſſiapiacke, which at that pꝛeſent we little er-
pected,hauing by a cruell ſtoꝛme bene put to the Noꝛthward:
anchoꝛing in this Bay twentie oꝛ thirtie went a ſhoꝛe with
the Captain,and in comming aboard,they were aſſalted with
certaine Indians,which charged them within Piſtoll ſhot:in
which conflict,Captaine Archer and Mathew Morton were
ſhot: wherupon, Captaine Newport ſeconding them,made a
ſhot at them,which the Indians little reſpected , but hauing
ſpent their arrowes retyꝛed without harme,and in that place
was the Boxopened,wherin the Counſell foꝛ Virginia was
nominated:and arriuing at the place where wee are now ſea-
ted,the Counſell was ſwoꝛne,the Pꝛeſident elected,which foꝛ
that yeare was Maiſter Edm. Maria Wingfield, where was

A 3   made

2. The title page of Captain John Smith's *The Generall Historie of Virginia, New-England, and the Summer Isles*, London, 1624. (The Tracy W. McGregor Collection of the Alderman Library, University of Virginia)

And here are no hard Landlords to racke vs with high rents, or extorted fines to consume vs; no tedious pleas in law to consume vs with their many years disputations for Iustice; no multitudes to occasion such impediments to good orders, as in popular States (I, 195–196; II, 710).

Smith therefore demands time for the ripening of the state under the rule of the competent. His splenetic attacks on idle "gentlemen" were not directed against aristocracy but against idleness—against a governing class derelict in its duties. In truth, there is a working relation between Bacon's essay on plantations and Smith's practical experience:

A child can neither performe the office, nor deedes of a man of strength, nor indure that affliction He is able; nor can an Apprentice at the first performe the part of a Maister. And if twentie yeeres bee required to make a child a man, seuen yeeres limited an apprentice for his trade, if scarce an age be sufficient to make a wise man a States man, and commonly a man dies ere he hath learned to be discreet: If perfection be so hard to be obtained, as of necessitie there must bee practice, as well as theorick: Let no man much condemne this paradox opinion, to say, that halfe seauen yeeres is scarce sufficient, for a good capacitie, to learne in these affaires, how to carrie himselfe: and who euer shall trie in these remote places the erecting of a Colony, shall finde at the ende of seauen yeares occasion enough to vse all his discretion: and, in the *Interim* all the content, rewardes, gaines, and hopes will be necessarily required, to be giuen to the beginning, till it bee able to creepe, to stand, and goe, yet time enough to keepe it from running: for there is no feare it wil grow too fast, or euer to any thing; except libertie, profit, honor, and prosperitie there found, more binde the planters of those affaires, in deuotion to effect it; then bondage, violence, tyranny, ingratitude

and such double dealing, as bindes freemen to become slaues, and honest men turne knaues: which
hath euer bin the ruine of the most popular com-
mon-weales; and is verie vnlikelie euer to begin in a
new (I: 215–216; II, 729–730).[15]

Controversy will ever rage over the authenticity
of *The True Travels, Adventvres, & Observations
of Captaine Iohn Smith* (1630), but the vitality of
the controversy is a measure of the vitality of the
first autobiography associated with American literature. It is idle to infer, as Smith's attackers have
done, that the wealth of laudatory verse at the opening of this volume is a mark of its egotism, inasmuch
as the same inference could be drawn regarding *The
Faerie Queen.* "To speake only of my selfe," writes
Smith in "The Epistle Dedicatory,"

were intolerable ingratitude; because, having had so
many co-partners with me; I cannot make a Monu-
ment for my selfe, and leave them unburied in the
fields, whose lives begot me the title of a Souldier;
for as they were companions with me in my dangers, so shall they be partakers with me in this
Tombe (II, 809).

The autobiography is, as a matter of fact, strewn
thickly with names, nor does Smith begrudge a noble
deed its meed of praise. An autobiography, to be interesting, must be egotistical, and it does not appear
that Smith is unduly self-absorbed. Suspicion arises,

---

[15] See in this connection the four-point preface to the *Generall
Historie,* with its frank appeal to authority: "If his [King James's]
Princely wisedome and powerfull hand, renowned through the world
for admirable government, please but to set these new Estates into
order; their composure will be singular: the counsell of divers is
confused; the generall Stocke is consumed; nothing but the touch of
the Kings sacred hand can erect a Monarchy" (I, 278).

however, from the ease with which he wins the al-
truistic attention of noble ladies no less than from a
fanciful geography which, in proportion as it is remote from England, has proved unverifiable; and
what is perhaps of deeper consequence, the work is
written in a variety of styles. Such a paragraph as
this may well pass as the honest reflection of a soldier
of fortune:

> But alas, what is it, when the power of Majestie
> pampered in all delights of pleasant vanity, neither
> knowing nor considering the labour of the Plough-
> man, the hazard of the Merchant, the oppression of
> Statesmen; nor feeling the piercing torments of
> broken limbes, and inveterated wounds, the toilsome
> marches, the bad lodging, the hungry diet, and the
> extreme misery that Souldiers endure to secure all
> those estates, and yet by the spight of malicious de-
> traction, starves for want of their reward and rec-
> ompences; whilst the politique Courtier, that com-
> monly aimes more at his owne honors and ends than
> his Countries good, or his Princes glory, honour, or
> security . . . (II, 846).

But an uneasy feeling that this is a touch too neatly
turned will not down; and a few pages later one
finds Smith in a debauch of rhetoric:

> Here *Busca* and the Emperour had their desire;
> for the Sunne no sooner displayed his beames, than
> the *Tartar* his colours; where at midday he stayed a
> while, to see the passage of a tryrannicall and treach-
> erous imposture, till the earth did blush with the
> bloud of honesty, that the Sunne for shame did hide
> himselfe from so monstrous sight of a cowardly
> calamity. It was a most brave sight to see the ban-
> ners and ensignes streaming in the aire, the glittering
> of Armour, the variety of colours, the motion of
> plumes, the forrests of lances, and the thicknesse of

shorter weapons, till the silent expedition of the
bloudy blast from the murdering Ordnance . . .
(II, 850).

This is not personal experience, but something in
King Cambyses' vein. The fact that the last third of
the book is composed of material "lifted" from
various sources for a makeweight suggests that the
True Travels was put together as a commercial job.
This does not negate the fascination of the opening
chapters, but it does, alas! prove that Smith was
usually addicted to invertebrate books. In the old
sense of the word he was a "projector," not a literary artist to whom the integrity of his work is
paramount, and it is in the first capacity that history
finds him so absorbing and so unreliable.

Only once (if he wrote it) did Smith create a perfect, albeit minute, literary production. For the most
part his verse is valueless; but at the opening of the
Advertisements For the unexperienced Planters is
printed an unsigned poem, "The Sea Marke," presumably his. No braggadocio mars this little lyric,
which is, as Emerson said of Allston's poems, "original and not conventional. The soul always hears an
admonition in such lines, let the subject be what it
may":

Aloofe, aloofe; and come no[t] neare,
          the dangers doe appeare;
Which if my ruine had not beene
          you had not seene:
I onely lie upon this shelfe
    to be a marke to all
    which on the same might fall,
That none may perish but my selfe.

If in or outward you be bound,
          doe not forget to sound;

Neglect of that was cause of this
>   to steare amisse.
The Seas were calme, the wind was faire
>   that made me so secure,
>   that now I must indure
All weathers be they foule or faire.

The Winters cold, the Summers heat
>   alternatively beat
Upon my bruised sides, that rue
>   because too true
That no releefe can ever come.
>   But why should I despaire
>   being promised so faire
That there shall be a day of Dome (II, 922).

Possibly the preserver of the Jamestown colony simply "borrowed" these lines, but it is pleasant to think of him as writing them in some moment of extraordinary spiritual insight.

A more practiced and conscious stylist (as befitted his wide culture), William Strachey,[16] though he

[16] William Strachey was apparently the son of William Strachey of Saffron Walden and, according to C. G. Culliford, his latest biographer, was probably born in 1572. In 1588 he became a pensioner at Emmanuel College and in 1595 he married. In 1606 he went to Constantinople as secretary to Sir Thomas Glover, was later dismissed, and returned to England. He seems to have been friendly with Donne, Campion, and Jonson. A member of the London Company, he sailed in the Gates expedition June 2, 1609, and was shipwrecked on the Bermudas. He reached Jamestown in May, 1610, and apparently wrote his account of the shipwreck while in Virginia. He was made secretary and recorder of the colony by Lord de la Warr, but he returned to London in 1611. Much of his literary work was done after that date. He died in 1621. See Culliford, *William Strachey, 1572–1621* (Charlottesville, 1965). For earlier accounts see Armistead C. Gordon, Jr.., in *DAB* and Charles Richard Sanders, "William Strachey, The Virginia Colony, and Shakespeare," *Virginia Magazine of History and Biography,* LVII (1949), 115–132.

Aside from some scattered verses, Strachey's first literary production was "A true repertory of the wracke, and redemption of Sir Thomas Gates Knight; upon, and from the Ilands of the Bermudas:

is said to have furnished Shakespeare with the shipwreck scene in *The Tempest,* has not figured as he
ought in American literature. Moses Coit Tyler, to be
sure, thought the "True Reportory" "a book of mar-
vellous power," but he devoted most of his discussion to quoting the description of the storm, the
style of which he called "magnificent— it has some
sentences which for imaginative and pathetic beauty,
for vivid implications of appalling danger and dias-
ter, can hardly be surpassed in the whole range of
English prose." [17] Tyler's enthusiasm is understand-
able, as anybody who reads the storm scene will see,
albeit the tempest is a rhetorical set piece for the
unknown "noble lady" to whom the document is ad-

---

his comming to Virginia, and the estate of that Colonie then, and
after, under the government of the Lord La Warre, July 15, 1610,"
first printed, apparently from manuscript, in *Purchas His Pilgrimes*
(see *ed. cit.,* XIX, 5–72). It has recently been reprinted in *A Voyage
to Virginia in 1609: Two Narratives, Strachey's "True Reportory"
and Jourdain's* Discovery of the Bermudas, ed. Louis B. Wright for
the Jamestown Documents series and published for the Association
of Virginia Antiquities by the University Press of Virginia (Charlottesville, 1964). For *The Colony in Virginia Britannia. Lawes
Diuine, Morall and Martiall, &c.* was published in London in 1612.
For later printings see p. 6, note 8. *The Historie of Travaile into
Virginia Britannia; Expressing the Cosmographie and Comodities of
the Country, Togither with the Manners and Customes of the People.
Gathered and Observed as well by those who went first thither as
Collected by William Strachey, Gent., The First Secretary of the
Colony* remained in manuscript until 1849, when it was first printed
under the editorship of R. H. Major for the Hakluyt Society. There
is a high degree of probability in Major's claim that Strachey also
wrote the "Letter from the Lord Delawarr, Governor of Virginia,
To the Patentees in England," signed by de la Warr and others (including Strachey), which he prints, pp. xxiii–xxxvi. Louis B. Wright
and Virginia Freund have edited a new edition of the *Historie of
Travell* for the Hakluyt Society (London, 1953).

[17] *A History of American Literature, 1607–1765* (New York,
1878), I, 42–45.

dressed, so that in the midst of the "swelling, and roaring" of the tempest Strachey pauses to observe:

> For surely (Noble Lady) as death comes not so sodaine nor apparant, so he comes not so elvish and painfull (to men especially even then in health and perfect habitudes of body) as at Sea; who comes at no time so welcome, but our frailty (so weake is the hold of hope in miserable demonstrations of danger) it makes guilty of many contrary changes, and conflicts: For indeede death is accompanied at no time, nor place with circumstances every way so uncapable of particularities of goodnesse and inward comforts, as at Sea (XIX, 6).

The careful distribution of assonance and alliteration in this passage is evident, just as Strachey's other rhetorical devices are evident a little later on: the shrieks of the women "made us looke one upon the other with troubled hearts, and panting bosomes: our clamours dround in the windes, and the windes in thunder"; the winds "(as having gotten their mouthes now free, and at liberty) spake more loud, and grew more tumultuous, and malignant"; the discovery of a leak meant that "we almost drowned within, whilest we sat looking when to perish from above"; and in the midst of the hurlyburly Sir Thomas Gates is made to utter a Latin pun.[18] These artifices get in the way of immediacy, and though they appealed to the seventeenth century, the twentieth is likely to find them a touch frigid.

The storm is none the less magnificent, but there are at least three othere elements in the "True Reportory" which also make it notable. Of these the

---

[18] "I have heard him say, wading out of the floud thereof, all his ambition was but to climbe up above hatches to dye in *Aperto coelo,* and in the company of his old friends" (XIX, 10).

basic one is a sense of structure: the narrative, from the departure out of Plymouth to the sailing of Sir Thomas Gates from Jamestown to England, is single; sunshine and storm are artfully distributed; and the account leads to its natural resolution and peaceful end:

And thus (right Noble Ladie) once more this famous businesse, as recreated, and dipped a new into life and spirit, hath raysed it (I hope) from infamy, and shall redeeme the staines and losses under which she hath suffered, since her first Conception (XIX, 67).

Even though the rhetorical method occasionally chills us by its artifice, we are in the hands of a skilled architect of prose. The second element is that not alone the storm, but life in the Bermudas and in Jamestown is graphically painted, not merely in small passages, like Lord de la Warr's landing, when he

fell upon his knees, and before us all, made a long and silent Prayer to himselfe, and after, marched up into the Towne, where at the Gate, I bowed with the Colours, and let them fall at his Lordship's feete (XIX, 59),

but in such another set piece as the formal description of Jamestown:

In the middest is a market place, a Store house, and a Corps du guard, as likewise a pretty Chappell, though (at this time when wee came in) as ruined and unfrequented: but the Lord Governour, and Captaine Generall, hath given order for the repairing of it, and at this instant, many hands are about it. It is in length threescore foote, in breadth twenty foure, and shall have a Chancell in it of Cedar, and a Communion Table of the Blake Walnut, and all the

Pewes of Cedar, with faire broad windowes, to shut
and open, as the weather shall occasion, of the same
wood, a Pulpet of the same, with a Font hewen hol-
low, like a Canoa, with two Bels at the West end.
It is so cast, as it be very light within, and the Lord
Governour and Captaine Generall doth cause it to be
kept passing sweete, and trimmed up with divers
flowers, with a Sexton belonging to it, and in it every
Sonday wee have sermons twice a day, and every
Thursday a Sermon, having true preachers, which
take their weekely turnes, and every morning at the
ringing of a Bell, about ten of the clocke, each man
addresseth himselfe to prayers, and so at foure of
the clocke before Supper. Every Sunday, when the
Lord Governour, and Captaine Generall goeth to
Church, hee is accompanied with all the Counsailers,
Captaines, other Officers, and all the Gentlemen, and
with a Guard of Holberdiers in his Lordships Livery,
faire red cloakes, to the number of fifty, both on each
side, and behinde him: and being in the Church, his
Lordship hath his seate in the Quier, in a greene Velvet Chaire, with a Cloath, with a Velvet Cushion
spread on a Table before him, on which he kneeleth,
and on each side sit the Counsell, Captaines, and
Officers, each in their place, and when he returneth
home againe, he is waited on to his house in the same
manner (XIX, 56–57).

What is convincing here is the details—the fair red
cloaks, the velvet cushion, the font like a canoe, the
windows that open and shut. These have been seen,
the report is personal, the itemization is convincing
and such as a man would notice in the wilderness. And
the third important element in the "True Reportory"
is that it is an argument (like that of Rolfe and John
Smith) against democracy and for a "more absolute
government" by those fitted to rule, who were of
course the gentlemen. The lessons of the Bermuda

shipwreck were twofold: on the one hand, because
the governor worked as hard as any other man, the
colonists grew "more diligent, and willing to be
called thereunto, where, they should see him before
they came"; and on the other hand, the three mutinies occurred because some of the people forgot their
due subordination. The result would have been an-
archy, "had wee not had a Governour with his authority, to have suppressed the same." Jamestown
but underlined the lesson:

> I have heard the inferioor people, with alacrity of
> spirit professe, that they should never refuse to doe
> their best in the practise of their sciences and knowl-
> edges, when such worthy, and Noble Gentlemen goe
> in and out before them, and not onely so, but as the
> occasion shall be offered, no lesse helpe them with
> their hand, then defend them with the Sword (XIX,
> 49).

Without the rule of the wise and good the "headlesse
multitude" necessarily fell into "neglect and sensuall
Surfet."

The *Lavves* of 1612, based in large measure on
Dale's enlargement of *Lawes for Governing the
Armye in the Lowe Countreyes* and published by
Strachey because men must learn "both how to
gouerne, and how to obey, (the end indeed of sociable
mankinds Creation)," were proof that "order and
gouernment" are "the onely hendges, whereupon, not
onely the safety, but the being of all states doe turne
and depend," and have already been touched upon.[19]
The Historie of Travaile into Virginia Britannia
is apparently all that remains of a much larger plan,

---

[19] See above, p. 6. The quotations above are from the prefatory
matter.

possibly a great history of the English in the New
World, of which but a preface and two books exist,
and even of these the second book degenerates into
annals. Strachey has brought immense learning to his
incompleted task, his pages bearing citations from
Camden, Gomara, Gilbert, Xenophon, Guicciardini,
Cicero, Acosta, Plutarch, Plautus, Festus, Paracelsus,
Pliny, Sir George Peckham, Plato, and a variety of
other worthies. He is also aware of scholasticism,[20]
and by no means ignorant of the stylistic devices of
his age.[21] He has woven Smith's *Map of Virginia,*

---

[20] "O let heavy things tend to their centre; let light and ayery
spiritts salute Heaven, and fly up to the circumference! . . . (As fier
worketh wood altogeather into fier), and as the eye, if it be opposed
and presented to any sensible object that excelleth, will loose his
proper and naturall function . . ." (p. 13). The Indians "are healthie,
which is *bonum corporis:* nor is nature a stepdame unto them con-
cerninge their *aptas membrorum compositiones;* only (God wot) I
must graunt, that *bonum morale,* as aforesaid, which is *per se,* they
have not *in medio,* which is *in virtute;* and then, how can they ever
obtayne yt *in ultimo,* which is *in fœlicitate?*" (p. 133) All references
are to the Hakluyt Society edition of 1849.

[21] Note the rhetorical pairing of adjectives at the opening of the
"Letter from the Lord Delawarr," p. xxiii; the alliteration of the
dedication to Bacon, as in "bound to your observaunce, by being one
of the Graies-Inne Societe"; "having bene there three yeares thither,
imploied in place"; "an inimitable patterne and perfecter"; "so
matchles a maister"; "opinionate worth of mine owne worke," etc.;
and the intricate rhythms of much of "A Præmonition to the Reader,"
which, in point of effort, is Strachey's most ambitious performance in
prose. E.g., "Alas, would we but truly examyne all, and the best of
things, which the rownd eye of the sun lookes uppon, what is the
travell for all the pompe, the treasure, the pleasure, and whatsoever
belongeth to this lief, compared to the ritches of the sowle, the ex-
cellency wherof (if there were noe other proufe to confirme yt) ys
suffycientlie sett fourth by the rich ransome that was paid for yt,
even the pretious bloud of Jesus Christ." The following sentence
carries a phrase like "eye-pleasing objects of our carnall sences"
compared to "poor Indian canoas" and a metaphor like that of fool-
ish men who "(like English lords) pursue these [objects] on the
streeme of delight, in swift barges" (pp. 16–17).

his own "True Reportory," and printed material
about the Popham colony into his own narrative. But
the result is curious and uneven. On the one hand,
Strachey appeals to the learned by quoting Plutarch
on Spartan food, Plautus to illustrate Indian appetite,
the Roman worship of the "hurtfull god Vejovis" as
an analogue to Indian religion, and Pliny's mention of
the Roman *favissae* to illuminate underground store-
houses in Virginia. On the other hand, he is not
merely bookish: he tells what he has seen and known,
or what he has learned from "one Kemps, an Indian,
who died the last yeare of the surveye[scurvy?],"
who told him the names of Powhatan's wives; Mac-
humps, another Indian, who at Sir Thomas Dale's
table, twice made grace offerings to the Indian god;
and the wife of one Pipisco, a Tapahannock Indian,
whom he visited:

I was once early at her howse (yt being sommer
tyme), when she was layed without dores, under the
shadowe of a broad-leaved tree, upon a pallett of
osiers, spred over with four or five fyne grey matts,
herself covered with a faire white drest deare skynne
or two; and when she rose, she had a mayd who fetcht
her a frontall of white currall, and pendants of great
but imperfect couloured and worse drilled pearles,
which she put into her eares, and a chayne, with long
lyncks of copper . . . which came twice or thrice about
her neck . . . and sure thus attired, with some variety
of feathers and flowers stuck in their haires, they seem
as *debonaire,* quaynt, and well pleased as (I wis) a
daughter of the howse of Austria . . . ; likewise her
mayd fetcht her a mantell, which they call puttawus,
which is like a side cloake, made of blew feathers, so
arteficyally and thick sowed togither, that it seemed
like a deepe purple satten, and is very smooth and
sleeke; and after she brought her water for her hands,

and then a braunch or twoo of fresh greene asshen leaves, as for a towell to dry them" (pp. 57–58).

Such a passage has great charm.

Nevertheless, Strachey fails to create a distinguished book because his ingredients do not fuse. The narrative parts are frequently flexible and easy, notably when he is rewriting an earlier narrative, but the "essay" parts or the passages of general discussion tend to garrulity. For the most part the Virginia section, or Book I, is superior to the New England portion—one supposes, because Strachey knew at first hand what he was writing about. He is notably good as an interpreter of Indian life, being both shrewd and sympathetic in his comments. There are likewise other flashes of insight, as in his remark that "all the low land of South and North Virginia is conjectured to have bene naturally gayned out of the sea," or his comment: "Yt yet maie be a probleme in philosophy whether variety of women be a furtherance or hinderer of manie birthes." But the difficulty is that even in Book I of *The Historie of Travaile* the individual elements, striking or excellent as they may be separately, do not add up into a vision of the world seen across a temperament, as is true of the less gifted but better integrated Smith. As for the second book, half as long as the first and obviously unfinished, the spirit goes out of it with the death of Popham in chapter vii, and the work dwindles into a brief Indian glossary. *The Historie of Travaile* is therefore a great work *manqué*.

Translator, secretary, letter writer, genteel vagabond, and *bon vivant*, John Pory [22] displays culture

[22] Son of William Pory, John Pory was born ca. 1570 in Norfolk; secured his B.A. at Gonville and Caius College, Cambridge, in 1591/2

and erudition comparable to that of William Strachey
and an activism paralleling that of John Smith and is

---

and his M.A. in 1595; and in 1610 was "incorporated" M.A. at Oxford. He studied with Hakluyt, and was later a friend of such anti-
quarians as Fulke Greville, Sir Robert Cotton, and J. Mead. His
one formal literary work, a translation of Leo Africanus (1600) is
obviously the result of his intercourse with Hakluyt. In 1605–10 he
was in parliament; in 1611–18 he traveled extensively in Ireland,
France, Italy, and Turkey, both as a private person and as a diplomatic attaché. During this period he served as an intermediary between English *savants* and such continental scholars as Isaac Casau-
bon and Jacques de Thou. A patentee (1609) of the Virginia charter,
he came to Jamestown April 19, 1619, where he was made secretary
and where he also served as speaker of the first legislative assembly.
Ousted from the secretaryship, he coasted New England, was
wrecked on the Azores, was captured by Spaniards and, barely escaping hanging, returned to England in 1623. He was chosen in 1623
a member of the commission to report on Virginia before the recall
of the patent, visiting the colony in 1624. He then settled in London,
dying in 1635. See the accounts by Miss C. Fell Smith in *DNB;*
Armistead C. Gordon, Jr., in *DAB;* Thomas Birch, *The Court and
Times of James the First* (London, 1848), *passim; Coll. Mass. Hist.
Soc.,* 4th ser., IX (1871), 11–21.

    The History and Description of Africa, translated by Pory as *A
Geographical Historie of Africa, Written in Arabicke and Italian
by Iohn Leo a More, borne in Granada, and brought vp in Bar-
barie . . . ,* first published in London, 1600, is accessible as nos. 92,
93, and 94 of the Hakluyt Society publications (London, 1896) and
was edited by Robert Brown, who, however, died before the edition
was completed. There is no edition of Pory's letters, which exist in
print in various states of mutilation and correctness in Birch, *Court
of James I* and *The Court and Times of Charles the First* (London,
1848); Susan Myra Kingsbury, ed., *The Records of the Virginia
Company of London,* III (Washington, 1933), *passim; Coll. Mass.
Hist. Soc.* cited above; and the historical magazines. For Pory's
minutes of the legislative assembly see above, pp. 8–10. In 1918
under the editorship of Champlin Burrage appeared *John Pory's Lost
Description of Plymouth Colony in the Earliest Days of the Pilgrim
Fathers* (Boston, 1918), which contains two "letters" by Pory. Note
should also be taken of three interesting letters by Pory (1618) concerning the execution of Sir Walter Raleigh reproduced in an article
by William S. Powell in *William and Mary Quarterly,* 3d ser., IX
(1952), 532–538.

humanly more amusing than either, albeit of lesser
stature. He had the antiquarian's love of gossip, his
relish for a touch of Latinity, his relish also for something faintly incredible as when he reports that two
Bristol men had "discovered an island where were
store of unicorns' horns, long and wreathed like that
at Windsor, which I have heard," he adds regretfully,
"to be nothing else but the snout of a fish," yet "pre-
cious against poison." [23] One of the ablest "Intelligenc-
ers" of the age, as Birch called him, his letters show
how completely the seventeenth-century epistle ful-
filled the function of the columnist and the special correspondent, compressing a great variety of news into
a single letter, news which came from the highest
sources, of course, and could not be contradicted until
the next letter. A worldly man with some repute for
winebibbing, he nevertheless enjoyed the confidence of
sober persons like Hakluyt and William Bradford, to
whom Pory's indignant Protestantism must have been
pleasing.[24] At the same time Pory was no zealot, and
moved easily in court circles, as a letter of 1632 to
Lord Brooke testifies:

On Saturday also, his majesty having taken cold
after he had heated himself at tennis, some red spots
appeared on his face and breast, which by Sunday
morning were converted into the smallpox. Yet the
queen (as I heard a Frenchman of the court affirm)
lay with him both these nights; and since, also, in the
daytime will never be out of his company. This disease
makes him not continually to keep his bed, but all the
day long he is up in a warm room, with a fur gown on

[23] Birch, *Court of Charles I*, II, 189.
[24] See in this connection the letters (*ibid.*, I, 119 ff.) on getting rid
of the French Catholic priests supposed to control the queen.

his back, and is merry, and eats and drinks heartily,
and recreates himself with some game or other.[25]

We rub our eyes. This is not the Merry Monarch of
Nell Gwynn's time as seen by Pepys, but the austere
Martyr, described by the pen of the man who wrote
William Bradford ten years earlier that the books
bestowed on Pory by Bradford and Brewster were
"juells," and who piously exclaimed:

And what good (who knows) it may please God to
worke by them, through my hands, (though most unworthy) who finds shuch high contente in them. God
have you all in his keeping.
> Your unfained and firme friend,
> John Pory [26]

Until such time as Pory's correspondence is prop-
erly assembled and printed we must rest content
with four literary documents from his pen. To the
first of these, the translation of Leo Africanus, Pory
brought scholarly geographical knowledge, some
knowledge of Italian, and a considerable knowledge
of Latin, which he sedulously concealed, inasmuch as
he professed to be using the Italian text but was really
employing a Latin "crib." He vastly admired Leo:

I maruell much how euer he should haue escaped so
manie thousands of imminent dangers. . . . For how
many desolate cold mountaines, and huge, drie, and
barren deserts passed he? How often was he in hazard to haue beene captiued, or to haue had his throte
cut by the prouling *Arabians,* and wilde Mores? And
how hardly manie times escaped he the Lyons greedie
mouth, and the deuouring iawes of the Crocodile? [27]

[25] *Ibid.*, II, 205. Birch modernized these letters.
[26] *Bradford's History of Plymouth Plantation* (Boston, 1912), I,
278–280.
[27] *The History and Description of Africa,* ed. cit., I, 6.

THE
Diſcoveries of JOHN LEDERER
from *Virginia* to the Weſt of *Carolina*,
and other parts of the Continent.

A General and brief Account of the North-
American *Continent.*

Orth, as well as South-*America*, may be di-
vided into three Regions : the Flats, the
Highlands, and the Mountains. The
Flats (in Indian, *Ahkynt*) is the Terri-
tory lying between the Eaſtern Coaſt, and
the falls of the great Rivers , that there
run into the *Atlantick* Ocean , in extent generally taken
Ninety miles. The Highlands (in Indian , *Ahkontſhuck*)
begin at thoſe falls, and determine at the foot of the great
ridge of Mountains that runs thorow the midſt of this Continent, Northeaſt and Southweſt, called by the Spaniards *A-*
palatæi, from the Nation *Apalakin*; and by the Indians, *Pæ-*
B   *motinck.*

---

which appertaine to our fetling there as Planters of a
Colonie,he is to make it his duty, to be a diligent not
onely ouer-feer,but labourer, himfelfe accompanying
therein, and feconding the example of his Captaine,
and induftrious Lieutenant,that the neceffary and daily
taskes of fuch workes and husbandry (without which
we cannot here keepe footing,nor poffibly fubfift) may
be in due time accomplifht and brought to paffe.

*Inftructions of the Marfhall for the better enabling
of a Serjeant to the exeuting of his charge in this pre-
fent Colonie,*Iune *the* 22. 1611.

Hat Captaine who fhall difpofe of a
Halbert,by vertue whereof a Serjeant is
knowne,ought to make choife of a man
well approoued,that hath paffed the in-
ferior grades,of a refolute fpirit, quick
apprehenfion, and actiue body,for it is
a place of great paines and promptitude, and that Serjeant who will be able to execute his duty in finceritie
and vprightneffe,muft not be flack to punifh where it
is deferued,nor ouer rafh to abufe his authority, vnbe-
fitting an officer of fuch moment.

This officer hath in the abfence of his fuperior officers the command of the company, to fee them doe
their duties,and obferue lawes and orders in all things,
and punifhment of them by his Halbert , or otherwife
in his difcretion, for defect or negligence in any part
of order.

This officer is to attend vpon the Serjeant Major for
the word vpon the fhutting in of the Ports, at the

K 3   Goue:

---

4. Opening page of the text of *The Discoveries of John Lederer,*
collected and translated by William Talbot, London, 1672. (The
Tracy W. McGregor Collection of the Alderman Library, University
of Virginia)

Here is the same Pepysian relish of life which appears
in the letters and which, in the translation, leads him
to linger on the icy fountains of Mount Atlas, the
Amazons, elephants, and the reason why the Cafri
are black.[28] But the translation was but preparation
for seeing the world, and the same delight in life appears in the letters which he wrote from Jamestown
in 1619:

> Nowe that yo[r] lo[p] may knowe, we are not the ver-
> iest beggers in the worlde, our Cowe-keeper here of
> Iames citty on Sundayes goes acowterd all in freshe
> flaming silkes and a wife of one that in England had
> professed the black arte not of a scholler but of a col-
> lier of Croydon, weares her rough beuer hatt wth a
> faire perle hattband, and a silken suite therto corre-
> spdent. But to leaue the Populace, and to come higher,
> the Gouerno[r] here, who at his first coming, besides a
> great deale of worth in his person, brought onely his
> sworde wth him, was at his late being in London, to-
> gether wth his lady, out of his meer gettings here, able
> to disburse very near three thousand pound to fur-
> nishe himselfe for his voiage.

The same correspondence shows him happily content
with the Horatian mean:

> At length being hardened to this custome of absti-
> nence from curiosity, I am resolued wholly to minde
> my busines here, and nexte after my penne, to haue
> some good book alwayes in store, being in solitude the
> best and choicest company. Besides among these
> Christall riuers, & odoriferous woods I doe escape
> muche expense, envye, contempte, vanity, and vexa-
> tion of minde.
>
> . . . *for I thanke god, I drinke water here wth as
> much (yf not more) pleasure & contente, as I dranke
> wine in those part[s].*

[28] See I, 16, 41, 63–64, 68, 75, 88.

. . . golden Medyum wch I hope will by proffitable vse verify ye sayinge *Medio tutissimus ibis.*[29]

Thus, amid his arguments for better vineyards, the importation of "sound persons," and thoughts about silk culture, Pory sounded the "note" of plantation life—*medio tutissimus ibis.*

Small wonder that a man so easily pleased became secretary of the first legislative assembly held in the future United States,[30] or that, finding the Cape Cod region as wonderful as Africa or Jamestown, he won the confidence of Bradford. His description of Plymouth, but recently come to light, has the same eagerness for life, the same relish for the unusual. Plymouth harbour was "not onelie pleasant for aire and prospect," but, "being landlocked on all sides," "most sure for shipping," and Bradford informed him that "for the space of one whole yeare, of the two wherein they had beene there, dyed not one man, woman, or child[!]" The eels practically caught themselves or obligingly bedded in gravel for winter digging; the bass and smelt were innumerable; the blue fish "excelleth all kinde of fish that ever I tasted"; and as for lobsters, a small boy caught enough for the ship's company in one hour, and clams were fed to the hogs. The Indians reported that oysters grew to be as "broad as a bushell," and one was as big as the ship's cabin, but the canny ship's captain was unimpressed by the antiquarian's argument: "If, said I, the oysters be soe greate and haue anie pearles in them, then must the pearles be answerable in greatnes to the oysters, and proving round and orient also, would farre

[29] Kingsbury, *op. cit.,* III, 221, 222, 256, 301.

[30] Pory's report, the third literary item to be associated with his name, is discussed above, pp. 5–6.

exceed all other jewells in the world!" [31] Pory's *Lost Description,* however romanticized, enables us to correct our too gloomy notions of Plymouth by the genial humor of the gentleman vagabond, whose notebook records admiration of a people who

both quietlie and justlie sate downe without either dispossessing anie of the natiues, or being resisted by them, and without shedding so much as one drop of blood, which faelicitie of theirs is confirmed unto them even by the voyces of the salvages them selues (p. 36). [32]

[31] *John Pory's Lost Description of Plymouth Colony,* pp. 37–41.

[32] *The Discovery of Nevv Brittaine . . . By Edward Bland, Merchant. Abram Woode, Captaine. Sackford Brewster, Elias Pennant, Gentlemen* . . . (London, 1651), reprinted by Sabin in New York (1873) and by Clarence W. Alvord and Lee Bidgood, *The First Explorations of the Trans-Allegheny Region by the Virginians, 1650–1674* (Cleveland, 1912), a short but forceful narrative, perhaps best belongs to the early literature of the Carolinas. At any rate, it is so brigaded by A. S. Salley, who reprints it in his *Narratives of Early Carolina* (New York, 1911), pp. 5 ff.

4. THE LETTER WRITERS

T HE ABSENCE OF A PRINTING PRESS [1] AND THEREFORE OF BOTH PAMPHLET AND NEWS SHEET ESTABLISHED THE MANUSCRIPT LETTER AS THE CHIEF medium of literary communication in seventeenth-century Virginia, a pattern of intellectual intercourse which lasted into the nineteenth century and which helps to explain why a figure like Jefferson turned naturally to letter writing rather than to book or essay for expression. The piety of descendants has printed innumerable seventeenth-century letters (with varying degrees of textual accuracy) in the historical magazines, though many others remain unpublished. The wanderer in this rich chaos finds a good many scattered passages of effective style, warm human interest, or unconscious humor. Sir Francis Wyatt castigating Captain Nathaniel Butler for his slanders against Virginia produced in 1623 or 1624 a piece of

---

[1] In 1682 John Buckner of Gloucester County brought the printer William Nuthead to Virginia, who printed a few sheets of the session laws of that year, but governmental action forced Nuthead to withdraw and Buckner to cease his support. William Parkes in 1730 established the first printing press in Virginia. See Douglas C. McMurtrie, *The Beginnings of Printing in Virginia* (Lexington, Va.), 1935.

epistolary sarcasm that has the right ring, as when he said: "This agrees with his finding devastations, where he never was, finding wrong judgment, where he never was present at the hearing and determining of causes, perhaps the cause of his malice"; but the modern reader is more likely to be startled by his statement: "To plant a Colony by water drinkers was an inexcusable errour in those, who layd the first foundacion, and have made it a received custome, which until it be laide down againe, there is small hope of health." [2] Or Alexander Murray, writing in 1665 from Mobjack Bay, expresses with considerable suavity what may be called the Horatian ideal:

Could a publick good, consist with a hermetik condi°n, I should prefere it before all others, but the nixt to it which is the settling in a wilderness of milk and honey: non can know the sweetness of it: but he that tasts it: one ocular inspection, one aromatik smel of our woods: one hearing of the consert of our birds in those woods would affect more than a 1000 reported stories let the authors be never so readible.[3]

And the gaiety of nations is increased by Nicholas Spencer's description of his state of health (1672):

My chiefe griefe is the paine of the Hypocondriacke, with some tymes A swiming in my head and A paine in the hinder part of it, with often moderate paines occationed as I suppose by wind flyeing into my shoulders, backe and hipps; little Appety, and little sleepe, often A nautiateing of my victualls; very subiect to receive coulds and apt to be A little feaverish. My urin is Thin, and pale. In A morning when I first rise I am apt to be troubled with A trembleing in my Limbs. By what I can understand of my distempers

---

[2] *William and Mary College Quarterly,* 2d ser., VI (1926), 114–121.

[3] *Ibid.,* II (1922), 157–161. Murray was a minister.

it proceeds from obstructions of spleen, Liver and Messeraicke veines.

"I beseech God," he says, to "sanctifie these afflictions unto me." [4] For the sake of brevity, however, three representative figures may be chosen for discussion. Even business letters are occasionally humanized, as when Frances Berkeley, writing to Robert Filmer, says that Filmer's widowed sister-in-law "likes this counterie so well she will not willinglie goe out of it." [5]

However repugnant the modern liberal may find the later career of Governor Sir William Berkeley,[6] his letters show him to have been a pungent stylist. Writing Sir Henry Bennet in 1665, he invents a phrase like "knowing that no seasonable showers or dews can recover a withered root"; and two years later, in an appeal to Arlington for financial assistance he says (having reference to court favors) : "I wanted the helpe of a frendly Angel to put me into the Poole

[4] *Ibid.,* III (1923), 134–136. Spencer survived. He was acting governor in 1684.

[5] Peter Walne, "Henry Filmer of Mulberry Island, Gentlemen," *Virginia Magazine of History and Biography,* LXVIII (1960), 408–428. The date is conjecturally 1670; the quoted phrase is on p. 427.

[6] Born 1606, the son of Maurice Berkeley of Bruton, Somersetshire, William Berkeley received his B.A. degree at Oxford in 1624, his M.A. in 1629, and made a career for himself as playwright, wit, and courtier. Knighted in 1639, he emigrated to Virginia in 1642, where he remained, save for a brief visit to England, until 1677. He was governor from 1641 to 1652 and again from 1660 to 1677, when he was recalled. He died without seeing the king July 9, 1677. See the account in *DAB* by Philip Alexander Bruce.

The Lost Lady. A Tragy Comedy was published in London, 1639, and seems to be Berkeley's solitary play. *A Discourse and View of Virginia* (London, 1663) was reprinted in a facsimile edition of 250 copies by William H. Smith (Norwalk, Conn., 1914). Berkeley's letters have not been collected. See above, pp. 10–11.

when the waters were made seasonable for hopes and powerful to heale dispayre." [7] Writing to England, he liked to picture himself as an old and broken man:

My Lord age and misfortune has wilted my desires as wel as hopes and the truth is I cannot in this time of my very old age so wish myselfe happy but that I presently repent of my desires to be so the way I proposed . . .

Sir,—I am so overwearied with riding into all parts of this Country to stop this violent rebellion that *I am not able to support myselfe at this Age six months longer and therefore on my knees I beg his sacred Majesty would send a more vigorous Governor,* [8]

but there was nothing feeble about the indomitable ancient who, at the age of 71, informed the Virginia commissioners that "Of this particular of the Postilions he is as innocent as the blessed Angels themselves," [9] and rejoiced evilly over the death of Nathaniel Bacon:

The justice and judgement of God overtooke him. His usual oath was here sworn (at least 1000 times a day was God damme my blood) and Gode soe infested his blood, that it bred lice in incredible numbers, so that for twenty days he never washt his shirts, but burned them. To this God added the bloody flux, and an honest minister wrote this epitaph upon him:

Bacon's dead. I am sorry at my heart
That lice and flux should act the hangman's part. [10]

[7] *Virginia Magazine of History and Biography,* XVIII (1910), 425; XXI (1913), 43.

[8] *Ibid.,* XXI (1913), 43; XVI (1908), 200.

[9] *Ibid.,* XXI (1913), 370. "Never saw the fellow's face but once before," he concludes roughly.

[10] *Ibid.,* XVI (1908), 200.

A savage, intemperate tyrant in his old age, he was an immensely active, loyal, fanatical, well-informed, dogmatical, and disillusioned proconsul.[11] Of his rough, military oratory something has already been said;[12] his pamphlet of 1663, *A Discourse and View of Virginia,* a piece of special pleading which bears the mark of haste but which displays nevertheless a statesmanlike grasp of the colonial problem, contains in a single sardonic sentence the key to his character:

> But a nearer way to a publick unquarrelled contribution they cannot find, having this Axiom firmly fixt in them, That never any Community of people had good done to them, but against their wills (8).

When for his cruelty the king finally recalled him, the old man, evil and incorruptible, might mournfully reflect on what he had written Arlington ten years earlier: 'I have donne the King and his blessed father all faithful service in my station, but am as farr from pretending merit to my King as the most pretending strict presbiterian is from [G]od." [13]

[11] See in this connection his clear and luminous letter to the king under date of August 1, 1665, telling of the fortifications Berkeley has built against the Dutch (XVIII [1910], 426); his excellent account of the Dutch attack (XX [1912], 134–140); and his vigorous prophecy of disaster to New England (XX [1912], 243–246) written in 1676. But see also two characteristic late letters printed by Wilcomb E. Washburn, "Sir William Berkeley's 'A History of Our Miseries,'" *William and Mary Quarterly,* 3d ser., XIV (1957), 403–413, and the editor's comments.

[12] See above, p. 10.

[13] XXI (1913), 43. The same letter, in which he asks for the customs on two hundred hogsheads of tobacco (he denounces tobacco growing in his pamphlet!) contains the characteristic observation that "though Ambition comonly leaves sober old age co[v]etuousness does not." Other quotations from unpublished letters by Berkeley may be read in Thomas J. Wertenbaker, *Virginia under the Stuarts, 1607–1688* (Princeton, 1914), *passim;* and in Alvord and Bidgood, *op. cit.,* pp. 175–179.

In comparison Thomas Ludwell [14] is a colorless figure, but he deserves to live in literature not so much for his smooth, official expository style [15] as for one or two passages of dramatic description. One of these concerns the Valley of Virginia:

[The explorers] were taken up by a river of (as they guesse) 450 yards wide, very rapid and full of rocks, running soe farr as they could see it due north between the hills, the bankes whereof were in most places, according to theire computation, nere one thos'd yards high, and soe broken that they could not coast it to give a more ample acc't of its progresse. The mountains they passed were high and rocky and soe grown w'th wood as gave them great difficulty to passe them, but from the last they were on, w'ch was at that river before menconed, they judged themselves w'thin ten miles of other hills, barren and naked of wood, full of broken white cliffs, beyond w'ch (soe long as they staid) they every morning saw a great fogg arise and hang in the aire till 10 o'clock; from whence we doe conjecture that those foggs arise either from morasse grounds or some great lake or river to w'ch those mountains give bound; and there we doe suppose will be the end of our labour, in some happy discovery w'ch we shall attempt in the end of Somer. [16]

[14] Born January 25, 1628/9, Thomas Ludwell, the son of Thomas and Jane Cottington Ludwell of Bruton, Somerset, probably came to Virginia with Berkeley in 1642; probably returned to England to fight for the king; came back to Jamestown; and after 1660 held various public offices. In 1675 he was one of three commissioners sent to England to rid the colony of proprietary grants. He died in Virginia, unmarried, October 1, 1678. See the sketch in Tyler, *Virginia Biography*, I, 126–127. His letters have not been collected.

[15] This may be seen in the letters printed in *Virginia Magazine of History and Biography*, IV (1897), 229–245; V (1897), 54–59; XX (1912), 19–21, 132–133, 357–359, etc.

[16] Ludwell to Arlington, June 27, 1670, *ibid.*, XIX (1911), 360–361, the punctuation modernized. The rest of the passage has to do with the hope that "the bowells of those barren hills are not w'thout

No other passage in the literature of seventeenth-century Virginia has thus quite caught the magic of natural distance.

Equally good is Ludwell's account of the hurricane of 1667:

But on the 27th of August followed the most dreadful hurricane that ever this country groaned under. It lasted 24 hours—began at North East and went round northerly till it came to West, and so on till it came to South East, where it ceased. It was accompanied with a most violent rain but no thunder. The night of it was the most Dismall tyme that ever I know or heard off, for the wind and rain raised so confused a noise, mixt with the continual cracks of falling houses and the murmur of the waves impetuously beaten against the shores and by that violence forced and, as it were, crowded up into all Creekes, Rivers and Bays to that prodigious height that it hazarded the drowning of many people who lived not in sight of the Rivers, yet were then forced to climb to the top of their houses to keep themselves above water. [It] carried all the foundations of the fort at Point Comfort into the river, and most of our Timber (which was very chargeably brought thither to perfect it). Had it been finished and a Garrison in it, they had been stormed by such an enemy as no power but God's can restrain, and in all likelyhood drowned, so that, had the lightening accompanied it, we should have believed nothing else from such a Confusion but that all the Elements were at strife which of them should doe most towards the reduction of the Creation into a second Chaos. It was wonderful to consider the contrary effects of that storm, for it blew some ships from their Anchors and carried them safe over shelves of sand where a Wherry could [with] difficulty pass, and

silver or gold, and that there are rivers falling the other way in to the sea as well as this to the east."

yet knockt the bottom [out] of a ship belonging to
Col. Scarbrough (ready to sail for England) in eight
foot water more than she drew. But when the morning
came, and the sun arisen, it would have comforted us
(or any else) after such a night, had it not withall
lighted us to ruins of our Plantations, of which I think
not one escaped. The nearest computation is at least
10,000 houses blown down, all the Indian Grain laid
flat upon the ground, all the Tobacco in the fields torn
to pieces and most of that which was in the houses
perished with them, the fences about the corn fields
either blown down or beaten to the ground by trees
which fell upon them; and before the owners could
repair them, the hogs and cattle got in, and in most
places devoured much of what the Storm had left
(and in many places all [was devoured]!), so that
we are at once threatened with the sword of the enemy returning upon us, with extreme wants of provision by the Storm, and of cloathes, ammunition and
other necessaries by the absence of the ships.[17]

This Defoelike realism, this grasp of what is visible
and tangible, this rapid reporting, are poles removed
from the conscious manner of Strachey.

The history of Virginia which William Fitzhugh [18]

[17] XIX (1911), 250–252, the punctuation modernized.

[18] Son of Henry Fitzhugh of Bedford, England, William Fitzhugh
was baptized January 10, 1651, emigrated to Virginia in 1670,
married in 1674, and acquired a large plantation in Stafford County.
An able lawyer, he defended George Beverly in 1683 against the
governor, and as a member of the House of Burgesses himself ex-
perienced political persecution in 1687. He served as lieutenant-colonel
of the Virginia militia. He died on October, 1701. There is a brief
biographical sketch in *DAB*.
His letters have been collected and printed in the *Virginia Magazine of History and Biography*, I (1893–94), 17–55, 105–126, 253–277,
391–410; II (1894–95), 15–36, 121–142, 259–275, 370–379; III (1895–
96), 1–15, 161–168, 253–261, 368–373; IV (1896–97), 67–74, 176–184,
310–312, 415–420; V (1897–98), 29–33, 169–173, 297–302. A better
edition is Richard Beale Davis, ed., *William Fitzhugh and His Chesa-*

"intended for the persuading Inhabitants hither" [19] was never written, and the digest of Virginia laws prepared by him has disappeared. Time has antiquated the learned expositions of legal precedents with which the published letters begin, and his account of tobacco shipments are mainly of interest to economists, but the chatty, garrulous plantation owner, type of gentleman farmer who came into being after the middle of the century, lives in his own right. Style gave him no end of trouble. "I must confess," he wrote Hayward in 1686, "I want abilitys, to polish & adorn my expressions with that Elegance & sweetness of Stile your two letters . . . are full freighted with" (p. 177), yet two years later he was censoring Durand's *Journal* for its formal defects:

I thank your kindness in Mr. Durands book & must agree with you, as well as I can understand it, that its a most weak unpolite piece, having neither the Rules of History, nor method of description, & taking it only as a private Gentleman's Journal, 'tis as barren & defective there too, when I come out in print do intend to appear more regular, & therefore as yet am not provided for such an undertaking (p. 245).

A sentence might wander endlessly through his pages,[20] but he was capable of terseness:

---

peake World: The Fitzhugh Letters and Other Documents (Virginia Historical Society, Vol. III; Chapel Hill, 1963; now distributed by the University Press of Virginia, Charlottesville), the source of the quotations printed here. The letters run from 1679 to 1697.

[19] See for the outline of the proposed work the letter to Nicholas Hayward, p. 224.

[20] See e.g., the opening of the letter to his brother of January 30, 1686/7 (p. 192). However, see also pp. 113–114, an example of legal loquacity.

The Widow says she has paid it, Capt. Brent says, he has never receiv'd it, one is my Neighbour & a Widow, the other is my particular friend (335).

Sometimes he labored an elaborate metaphor:

With the same Content & satisfaction as wearyed travellers take up their Inn, or weather beaten Voyagers their desired Port, after a long tedious & stormy voyage, so did I the most welcome joyfull, & glad news of your health, welfare, & prosperity (pp. 170–171).

But sudden picturesqueness is more characteristic, as when he speaks of "good hearty plantable land," "a skilfull & quaint Surgeon," "a warm wary person." Occasionally he is innocently comical, as in this letter to his brother in 1686:

God almighty hath been pleased to bless me with a very good wife, & five pledges of our conjugall affection, three of which he has been pleas'd to call into the arms of his mercy, & lent me two a hopefull boy & girle, & one other that will not suffer so close confinement, is preparing to come into the world (p. 171).[21]

He gives us also the homely details of plantation life, as when he scolds John Buckner for selling him a dumb Negro woman—"you knew her quality," he says, "which is bad at work worse at talking, & [you] took the opportunity of the softness of my Messenger, to quit your hands of her" (p. 105), or protests to a Mrs. Letten, an exasperating woman:

[21] This seemed to him so good he tried it again: "I have now been married this thirteen years, in which time God has blessed me with six dear Pledges of Conjugall Affections, two sons one daughter I am well assured are Angels in Heaven, & the same quantity & of like quality I now enjoy to my great comfort & satisfaction" (p. 200).

Now Madam having thus clearly laid down the matter to you, I must request you to call reason to the helm before you give your Censure, & consider where the fault lyes (p. 315).

He cannot forego a sardonic hit at his own family:

Your letter to my brother Luke he receiv'd but the meaning thereof my sister being dead, he will not be made to understand at present, & is so great a fool, that in one years time he will be incapable of serving himself or friends, therefore I advise if he owes you anything, you take the first opportunity, while he has something left, to get it out of his hands (p. 336).

One of the more amusing notes apologizes for being drunk:

I cannot miss this opportunity to beg my Excuse for parting so rudely without taking leave, I am sure some of the company were equally concerned, in the Bacchanalian Banquet, & those that were not cannot deny an Excuse to the great absurdity, or Solecisms committed by Bacchanals, who have Priviledge for them by Bacchus himself, the first Institutor of the Order (pp. 94–95).[22]

One reads Fitzhugh for these strokes of humanity, but he is even more useful as illustrating the growth of neoclassical culture. A contemporary of Dryden, he could turn a moral sentiment as neatly as Dick Steele:

By my Sister I understand our poor Mother & dear Sister, have not only tasted, but drank a large draught of the Cup of Affliction, & waded thro' abundance of Calamitys & troubles, which I truly condole, & do think it both our dutys, not only to commiserate, but as far as our abilitys extend, not to suffer one to want,

---

[22] Fitzhugh thriftily repeats the metaphor in a letter to Hayward (p. 205). Note also the repetition of the figure of the miser and his money bags, pp. 189 and 214.

who gave us our being, nor suffer her to strugle to
live, who (under God) gave us life here. Charity di-
rects to help those in want & distress, but nature,
duty, the Laws of God and Man, not only commands
but enjoins, to give the utmost help to a distressed
Parent (p. 171).[23]

"Afflictions," he tells his parent, "mature & ripen the
soul for heaven" (p. 197), but he found utility a more
practical guide. "I know," he wrote Richard Lee in
1687/8,

you are too well practised in the Topicks of Honour
& generosity, to render advice other than fair and
Candid, & . . . you are not Yorkshire enough, to set
the Course of your advice by the Compass of your Interest. Sir I shall always endeavour to manage those
parts that God Almighty have given me the use of,
that the Devil may not have the application, & to be
sure to keep honesty & integrity at the helm, when I
launch out into any manner of Concerns (p. 235).[24]

But his most striking rule of conduct, the ideal which,
guiding other Virginians (as has been seen), was central in the life of Fitzhugh was the Horatian doctrine
of the mean:

> Beatus ille qui procul negotiis,
> Ut prisca gens mortalium,
> Paterna rura bobus exercet suis,

[23] The sentiment was sincere. A series of letters to and about his
mother testify to Fitzhugh's filial affection. There is a pathetic line in
a letter to John Cooper (May 17, 1695) which reveals how at the
mercy of events was the colonial correspondent: "I have not had a
line from my mother now this two year & upwards" (p. 331). When
communication was reopened, he had been extremely ill himself and
a favorite sister had died (pp. 333–335).

[24] Yet he wrote Hayward January 30, 1686/7, deploring "the want
of spirituall help & comforts, of which this fertile Country in every
thing else, is barren and unfruitfull" (p. 203).

Solutus omni faenore,
Neque excitatur classico miles truci,
Neque horret iratum mare,
Forumque vitat et superba civium
Potentiorum limina.

Fitzhugh returns again and again to the doctrine of the just withdrawal, the quiet happiness of avoiding strife:

Praised be God I neither live in poverty nor pomp, but in a very good indifferency, & to a full content (p. 173).

I never met a Disapointment with greater chearfullness, than when I was informed of your [Hayward's] . . . Purchase of the seat of land contiguous, for my intention of purchase was to have such neighbours on it, as might live quietly & honestly, the contrary of which are in all places ill, but here really pernicious (p. 177).

. . . contented Condition, which in my opinion far exceeds the other [that of wealth], for its the mark that all drive at, from the Monarch on the Throne, to the lowest Tradesman, without which the Riches of Croesus are not satisfactory, & with it the lowest Degree passes his time away here pleasantly (p. 200).

As your late purchased Villa gives you the happy opportunity of a retirement, so it gives at the same time the secret & pleasant enjoyment of your self & a true Epicurean contentment, that is, a reall satisfaction of the mind, which I heartily & sincerely wish you (p. 314).

Such was this honest Virginian, who, if he wrote that "kind husbands may be sometimes met with, but to meet with a concatenation of an Indulgent Husband, an obliging nature, and generous temper in one person is very rare" (p. 199), could also lament that

"our Estates here depend altogether upon Contin-
gencys" which "exceed my Inclinations in worldly affairs" (p. 203), and in one and the same letter ask
for "an ingenious boy out off the Hospital" to "cast
accounts" and for "an able, learned, serious & sober
Minister whose allowance here would be large, &
comfortable" (p. 268). When he died, Jamestown
was almost a century old. His kindly, rambling correspondence reflects a culture which, if it lack the finer
ornaments, is sure of itself and not inclined to great
exertions.

5. THE LITERATURE OF THE SECOND HALF-CENTURY

IN THE SECOND HALF OF THE SEVEN-TEENTH CENTURY THE LITERA-TURE OF VIRGINIA TENDED TO FO-CUS UPON THREE MAJOR THEMES— THE FURTHER EXPLORATION OF THE land, the economic future of the colony, and the great political upheaval known as Bacon's Rebellion. The romance of the Jamestown settlement has tended to obscure the later progress of discovery; and, truth to tell, most of the subsequent narratives lack the picturesque and dramatic detail which gives perennial interest to the writings of John Smith and his contemporaries.[1] Nevertheless, the accounts of at least two

[1] The letters of Captain Thomas Yong regarding his exploration of the Delaware River belong to the literature of Maryland, despite the long account of Virginian life in the first of these. See below, note 2. *An Account of Virginia, its Scituation, Temperature, Productions, Inhabitants and their manner of planting and ordering Tobacco . . .* by Thomas Glover, "an ingenious Chirurgion that hath lived some years in that Country," originally printed in the *Philosophical Transactions [of the Royal Society]* (June 20, 1676) and thence reprinted by B. H. Blackwell (Oxford, 1904) in an edition limited to 250 copies, exhibits a good deal of medical lore and contains an admirable paragraph on the mockingbird: "As to the *Mocking-bird,* besides his own natural notes, which are many and pleasant, he imitateth all the birds

of these later writers are of absorbing interest; and the narratives of two other, but lesser, explorers show in occasional moments how well the language can be written by practical men.

The text of the first of these exists in two states,[2] but the version to be preferred is that in the first per-

---

in the woods, from whence he taketh his name; he singeth not only in the day, but also at all hours in the night, on the tops of the Chimneys; he is strangely antick in his flying, sometimes fluttering in the air with his head down and tail up, other times with his tail down and head up; being kept tame, he is very docible" (p. 20). The rattles of the rattlesnake are "a peculiar providence of God to warn people" (p. 21), but on the whole this pamphlet is not striking. The letters of John Banister (*Phil. Trans.*, XVII [1694], 667–672) can be praised only by those who have not read them critically. Likewise without literary merit is Cuthbert Potter's "Journall and Narrative of a Journey . . . from Virginia to . . . New England [1690]" reprinted in Newton D. Mereness, *Travels in the American Colonies* (New York, 1916), pp. 4–11.

[2] "A Journal from Virginia Beyond the Appalachian Mountains in Septr., 1671, Sent to the Royal Society by Mr. Clayton, and read Aug 1, 1688, before the Said Society," as this is reprinted in the *William and Mary College Quarterly*, 1st ser., XV (1907), 234–241, is in the first person and is reprinted in Berthold Fernow, *The Ohio Valley in Colonial Days* (Munsell's Historical Series no. 17; Albany, 1890), pp. 220–229; and in Alvord and Bidgood, *op. cit.*, pp. 183–195. The first-person version also appears in *The Reverend John Clayton: A Parson with a Scientific Mind,* ed. Edmund and Dorothy Smith Berkeley (Virginia Historical Society Documents, Vol. VI; Charlottesville, 1965), pp. 68–77, where it is said to be taken from a manuscript in the British Museum, Sloane MSS 4432, f.9. Quotations in the text are from the *Quarterly*. Entitled "The Journal & Relation of a New Discovery made behind the Apulein Mountains to the West of Virginia," the same material in the third person and otherwise altered is found in *Documents Relative to the Colonial History of the State of New York* (Albany, 1853), III, 193–197 (ed. John R. Brodhead). The source of this version is said to be "Plantations General Papers, I: 21." According to the Berkeleys in their collection of Clayton's writings, this third-person transcript was made by Dr. Daniel Coxe, author of *A Description of the English Province of Carolana, etc.* (London, 1722).

son. In September, 1671, Thomas Batts, Thomas
Wood, Robert Fallam, an Indian named Perecute,
and a serving man left Appomattox with the purpose
of "finding out the ebbing and flowing Water on the
other side of the Mountains, in order to the discovery of the South Sea." The authorship of their journal is uncertain, but the writer, whoever he was, exhibits a delight in wild nature supposed to be reserved
for the romanticists:

It was a pleasing tho' dreadful sight to see the Mountains and Hills as if piled one upon another.

He speaks also of "curious meadows on each side" of
the trail, "curious rising hills and brave meadows
with grass above man's height" visible from the
mountain tops. "As we marched," he says,

in a clear place at the top of a hill we saw ag^t us lying
south West a curious prospect of hills like waves
raised by a gentle breese of wind rising one after another. Mr Batt supposed he saw houses: but I rather
think them to be white Cliffs.

Turned back by illness, the explorers leave us an un-
forgettable glimpse of the beckoning west:

We returned homewards, and when we were on the
Top of the hill, we turned about and saw over against
us westerly over a certain delightfull hill a fog arise,
and a glimmering light as from Water. We suppose
there to be a great Bay.[3]

The Discoveries of John Lederer (1672)[4] is a

[3] *William and Mary College Quarterly,* 1st ser., XV (1907), 238,
239, 241.
[4] *The Discoveries of John Lederer, In three several Marches from
Virginia, To the West of Carolina, And other parts of the Continent.
Begun in March 1669, and ended in September 1670* (London, 1672)

much more substantial work, albeit the author is almost as shadowy as the writer of the preceding journal. Lederer's three journeys were directed towards finding the South Sea passage ("the long looked-for discovery," says Sir William Talbot in the introduction, "of the Indian Sea does nearly approach"), the Appalachians rising against the explorers like "the prodigious wall that divides China and Tartary." The sense of horror and fascination of the wilderness is again vividly expressed:

The fifteenth of March, not far from this hill, passing over the South-branch of Rappahanock-river, I was almost swallowed in a quicksand. Great herds of red and fallow deer I daily saw feeding; and on the hill-sides, bears crushing mast like swine. Small leopards I have seen in the woods, but never any lions, though their skins are much worn by the Indians. The wolves in these parts are so ravenous, that I often in the night feared my horse would be devoured by them, they would gather up and howl so close round about him, though tethr'd to the same tree at whose foot I my self and the Indians lay: but the fires which we made, I suppose, scared them from worrying us all. Beaver and otter I met with at every river that

has been reprinted; once in an edition of 300 copies for George P. Humphrey (Rochester, 1902); once in Alvord and Bidgood, *op. cit.,* wherein it appears on pp. 131–171. These editors refer to a Cincinnati reprint by Harpel, edited by H. A. Rattermann, which I have not seen. The latest reprint seems to be *The Discoveries of John Lederer with unpublished letters by and about Lederer to John Winthrop, Jr., and an Essay on the Indians of Lederer's* Discoveries *by Douglas L. Rights and William P. Cumming.* This was edited by Cumming and published by the University of Virginia Press in collaboration with the Tracy C. McGregor Library and the Wachovia Historical Society at Charlottesville in 1958. Quotations in the text are from the Humphrey reprint, the source of the Alvord-Bidgood version. The original was written in Latin. What little is known of Lederer's biography may be read in the account in *DAB* by Fred W. Shipman.

I passed; and the woods are full of grey foxes (p. 11).

He found the air of the mountains "very thick and chill," their streams had a "blue colour, and allumish taste," and the precipice he climbed was so steep "that if I lookt down, I was immediately taken with a swimming in my head," albeit he later admired the "beautiful prospect of the Atlantick-Ocean washing the Virginian-shore." On his third expedition he found "Savanae," their verdure "wonderful pleasant to the eye, especially of such as having travelled through the shade of the vast forest, come out of a mela[n]choly darkness of a sudden, into a clear and open skie" where there were "flowry meads" supporting innumerable red deer, and elk, which fed by dropping on their knees.[5] At first impressed by Indian culture,[6] the more he penetrated the wilderness, the

[5] Lederer describes one occurrence which might have helped the hard-pressed Audubon to defend his picture of a snake climbing a tree. The Indians told him it was usual for rattlesnakes, "when they lie basking in the sun, to fetch down these squirrels from the tops of the trees, by fixing their eye steadfastly upon them; the horrour of which strikes such an affrightment into the little beast, that he has no power to hinder himself from tumbling down into the jaws of his enemy, who takes in all his sustenance without chewing, his teeth serving him onely to offend withal. But I rather believe what I have heard from others, that these serpents climb the trees, and surprise their prey in the nest" (p. 10).

[6] "Though they want those means of improving human reason, which the use of letters affords us; let us not therefore conclude them wholly destitute of learning and sciences: for by these little helps which they have found [mnemonic devices], many of them advance their natural understandings to great knowledge in physick, rhetorick and policie of government: for I have been present at several of their consultations and debates, and to my admiration have heard some of their seniors deliver themselves with as much judgement and eloquence as I should have expected from men of civil education and literature" (p. 9).

more horrified he grew. One Indian tribe sent three young men to scalp three girls from the enemy tribe so that the king's son should be served in the other world; in another an Indian boy shot an arrow through Lederer's clothing; and among the Ushery Indians he saw incredible things:

These miserable wretches are strangely infatuated with illusions of the devil: it caused no small horrour in me, to see one of them wrythe his neck all on one side, foam at the mouth, stand bare-foot upon burning coals for near an hour, and then recovering his senses, leap out of the fire without hurt or signe of any. This I was an eye-witness of (p. 21).

A fine topographer, whose general account of eastern America is excellent, Lederer came to believe that a bay might indent the California coast somewhere on the western mountain slope but that no river flowed from the Appalachians into the Indian Ocean. In his able pamphlet one catches the full flavor of the appeal of the vast and trackless western wilderness to one who found the settled shores of Virginia tame and unprofitable.[7]

These minor accounts are, as it were, compounded of adventure and natural history; the two major writers yet to be considered divide these themes between them. Why Norwood's *Voyage to Virginia*[8] is not

[7] Other but minor travel accounts by John Clayton (for Batts and Fallam) and Abraham Wood (for Neadham and Arthur) appear in Alvord and Bidgood, *op. cit.*, pp. 183 ff. Reprinting an anonymous manuscript in the Ayer Collection of the Newberry Library, Stanley Pargellis, "An Account of the Indians in Virginia," *William and Mary Quarterly*, 3d ser., XVI (1959), 228–243, suggests it may have been written by John Clayton.

[8] Although Sabine lists the original as "n. p., n. d., 8 vo. pp. 50," this narrative is best known by its appearance in A. Churchill's *A Collection of Voyages and Travels, Some Now first Printed from*

better known to lovers of good narrative must remain a mystery. Almost the first full-blooded adventure story in American literature (for Norwood's whole interest is simply in saving his skin and the lives of his associates), the *Voyage to Virginia* is a kind of cross between Daniel Defoe and Samuel Pepys— Defoelike in its verisimilitude, Pepysian in its exposure, innocent or self-conscious, of the inconsistencies of human nature. Of questionless courage and unlimited endurance, the author, who volunteered to swim from island to mainland (after the abandoning of the ship's passengers) in order that the Indians, if he could find any, should either succor them or destroy him—the author seems to delight in celebrating his own selfishness. On shipboard, with passengers dying daily from thirst, Norwood and the captain of the vessel secretly drank claret or got water or the lees of wine out of empty casks for themselves. One of three shipwrecked women "had the envied happiness to die"; whereupon Norwood advised the other two to eat her, "as they did to good effect." Before the little group was rescued, Norwood, going off by himself, killed a goose, which he resolved to eat alone, but, hanging it temporarily in a tree, he found that

---

Original Manuscripts, Others Now first Published in English. In Six Volumes. Quotations in the text are from Vol. VI of the third edition of Churchill (London, 1744–46), pp. 161–186. This was reprinted as no. 10, Vol. III of the Force *Tracts;* and an unskillful condensation appears in the *Virginia Historical Register and Literary Advertiser,* ed. William Maxwell, II (1849), 121–137. Little is known of Norwood's biography. See, however, Fairfax Harrison, "Henry Norwood (1615–1689)," *Virginia Magazine of History and Biography,* XXXIII (1925), 1–10; and J. H. Trye, "Colonel Henry Norwood of Lockhampton, Co. Gloucester," in *Transactions of the Bristol and Gloucestershire Archaeological Society,* XLVII (1925), 113–121.

the "wolves" had stolen it, whereupon he moralizes in this manner:

The Loss of this goose, which my empty stomach look'd for with no small hopes of satisfaction, did vex me heartily. I wish'd I could have taken the thief of my goose to have serv'd him in the same kind, and to have taken my revenge in the law of retaliation. But that which troubled me more, was an apprehension that came into my mind, that this loss had been the effect of divine justice on me, for designing to deal unequally with the rest of my fellow-sufferers; which I thought, at first blush, look'd like a breach of trust: but then again when I consider'd the equity of the thing, that I did it merely to enable myself to attain their preservation, and which otherwise I could not have done, I found I could absolve myself from any guilt of that kind (VI, 174).

When the Indians ("angels of light," says Norwood) made him the present of the leg of a swan he "eat as privately as it was given me," but this same worldly cavalier took his turn at the pump, found it "a wonderful mercy" that his legs remained "in competent strength" on the island, resolved to employ them "for our common good . . . by God's help . . . to the last gasp," emerged immediately as the leader of the shipwrecked band, and was so regarded by the Indians:

They did me the honour to make all applications to me, as being of largest dimensions, and equip'd in a camlet coat glittering with galoon lace of gold and silver, it being generally true, that where knowledge informs not, the habit qualifies (VI, 175).

He was the stuff to arouse passionate loyalty in common men:

At the time I quitted the ship my servant *Thomas Harman,* a *Dutchman,* did at parting advertise me

(for I left him on board to look to my goods), that in
the bundle I ordered to be carry'd with me on shore,
I should find about thirty bisket cakes, which he, by
unparallel'd frugality, had saved out of his own belly
in the great dearth and scarcity we lived in. The
thoughts of these biskets entring upon me at the time
I was press'd to accept this charge [i.e., the command
of the shipwrecked party], I thought myself obliged
in christian equity, to let every one partake of what I
had; and so dividing the bread into nineteenth parts
(which was our number) perhaps I added the frac-
tion to my own share (VI, 171).[9]

A gentleman despite his self-disparagement, Norwood
honored courage and goodness when he saw it; amid
the horrors of shipwreck he says of two foremast-
men, Thomas Reasin and John Smith, "men of innate
courage," that "for their good resolution on that and
divers other occasions in the various traverses of this
voyage," they "deserve to have their names kept in
lasting remembrance." The kindness of the natives
led Norwood to reflect bitterly upon the inhumanity
of coastal dwellers in Britain towards the shipwrecked
and to write:

   . . . on the contrary, our charitable [Indian] host,
influenced only by natural law, without the least shew
of coveting any thing we had, or prospect of requital

   [9] This tribute to Norwood is the more remarkable after the ghastly
indiscipline on *The Virginia Merchant* ("untruly so call'd," says
Norwood grimly), whose captain abandoned the passengers to their
fate. The boat first struck just as the mate had refused a drink of
brandy and had said "he would look out to see what change there
was in the water." "The seamen were soon on deck with this dismal
alarm, and saw the cause thereof; but instead of applying their hands
for their preservation (through a general despondency) they fell on
their knees, commending their souls as at the last gasp. The captain
came out at the noise to rectify what was amiss; but seeing how the
case stood, his courage failed" (VI, 164).

in the future, did not only treat in this manner our persons, but did also, with as much honesty, secure for us our small stores of guns, powder, *&c.* as if he had read and understood the duty of the gospel, or had given his only child as a hostage to secure his dealing justly with us; so that I can never sufficiently applaud the humanity of this *Indian,* nor express the high contentment that I enjoyed in this poor man's cottage, which was made of nothing but mat and reeds, and bark of trees fix'd to poles. It had a loveliness and symmetry in the air of it, so pleasing to the eye, and refreshing to the mind, that neither the splendor of the *Escurial,* nor the glorious appearance of *Versailles* were able to stand in competition with it (VI, 177).

In truth, the ending of the adventure has all the right goodness in it: an Indian queen "so gentle and compassionate, as did very bountifully requite all defects of nature," prepared a penultimate entertainment in the primitive woods, which is still savory across wellnigh three hundred years:

The lusty rousing fire, prepared to warm me, would have been noble entertainment of itself, but attended (as it was quickly) with good food for the belly, made it to be that compleat good chear I only aimed at; a wild turkey boiled, with oysters, was preparing for my supper, which, when it was ready, was served up in the same pot that boiled it. It was a very savoury mess, stew'd with muscles [i.e., mussels], and I believe would have passed for a delicacy at any great table in *England,* by palates more competent to make a judgment than mine, which was now more gratify'd with the quantity than the quality of what was before me (VI, 182).

"And thus," concludes this eupeptic narrative,

(by the good providence of a gracious God, who helpeth us in our low estate, and caused his angels to pitch tents round about them that trust in him) have I given as faithful an account of this signal instance of his goodness to the miserable objects of his mercy in this voyage, as I have been able to call to a clear remembrance (VI, 186).

Norwood's *Voyage* is the literary masterpiece of the second half of the century in Virginia—a more unified piece of writing than anything by Smith, however much it lacks in public import. It is also the mirror of a frank, humorous, manly, and unashamed personality, in which the natural man is not altogether hidden beneath the mundane humors of the cavalier.

No greater contrast in tone and substance to Norwood's *Voyage* can be imagined than the letters which the Rev. John Clayton [10] contributed to the Royal Society or wrote to such excellent naturalists as Dr. Nehemiah Grew. Clayton, who left Virginia in 1686, was not averse to relating an anecdote:

Mr. *Wormley,* one of the Council of State in *Virginia,* told me, that being in Company with another Gentleman, he had an Opportunity of making the following Experiment; for seeing a *Rattlesnake* in her Coil,[11] they went and got a Bunch of this *Dittany,* and tied it to a Pole; then putting the *Dittany* that was thereon to the Nose of the *Snake,* it seemed to offend her, whereupon she turned away her Head, which

[10] *Phil. Trans.,* XVII (1694), 781-795, 941-948, 978-999; XVIII (1695), 121-135; XLI, pt. i (1744, for the years 1739-40), 59-61, 143-162, 162-166. There is also an interesting letter from Clayton to Dr. Nehemiah Grew (?) in *William and Mary College Quarterly,* 2d ser., I (1921), 114-115. The Royal Society letters printed in 1694-95 were reprinted in the Force *Tracts,* Vol. III, no. 12. The later letters were sent to Grew and found their way into the *Phil. Trans.* through the Earl of Egmont. Clayton's letters may also be found in *The Reverend John Clayton* (p. 87, note 2).

[11] The rattlesnake, he says elsewhere (*Phil. Trans.,* XVIII, 127), "is a very Majestick sort of Creature."

they still followed with the *Dittany;* then the *Snake* fled, and they still pursuing her, she at last stretched herself out at Length, and lay seemingly dead. Then they laid the *Dittany* upon her Head, and went into a neighbouring House to refresh themselves; for they were tired with skipping about after the *Snake.* When they had staid near half an Hour, they returned to see their supposed dead *Snake;* but, behold! the *Snake* was fled; so that they had then judged, that the *Snake* had only stretched herself out because she had been tired with their Pursuit (XLI, pt. i, 154).

The unexpected light upon the bibulous habits of the Virginians is not, however, the point of this story, which is designed to show that dittany does not kill snakes; and it is evident from Clayton's letters that, long before Franklin, he had resolved to make the *useful* his aim in life. In him, accordingly, the naturalist and the objective observer are joined with the utilitarian; on the one hand, he will admit nothing into his pages which cannot be rationally accepted,[12] and on the other hand, his notes on men and nature and his own actions are consistently directed towards practical ends. He observed that in Virginia horses could be worked without shoes because of the good roads, the result of oyster shells being mixed in with earth; that tobacco seeds being kept in a decoction,

---

[12] These two passages are characteristic: " 'Tis commonly asserted by the Seamen, that they can smell the Pines at *Virginia* several Leagues at Sea before they see Land, but I could receive no satisfaction as to this Point; I could not discern any such thing when at a moderate distance, I fear much of this may be attributed to Fancy" (XVII, 783). "There's a Tradition amongst them, that the Tongue of one of these Woodpeckers dryed will make the Teeth drop out if pick'd therewith, and cure the Tooth-ach tho' I believe little of it, but look on it as ridiculous; yet I thought fit to hint as much that others may try; for sometimes such old Stories refer to some peculiar Vertues, tho' not to all that is said of them" (XVII, 991–992).

they "came up much sooner, grew swifter, and I had five Plants for one more than any of the other Beds"; that on the plantation where he lived (owned by "a very Acute Ingenious Lady") he drained the swamp lands in thirteen days, a matter on which he had previously "discoursed it very warmly," the results being good; and, persuading the same lady to milk her four cows during the winter instead of letting them run wild, "she found so good Effect, that she assured me she would keep to my Advice for the future." A busy, active, pottering sort of man, having as many projects as Defoe's academy, irresistibly led from cattle to clay and from clay to pottery, he must handle, feel, touch, and weigh before he is convinced. "I have Anatomized most sorts of Creatures, and never found any Four-footed Creature with an Ear like a Bird, unless a Mole," he writes à propos of dissections to discover how birds sing; yet, "having no Skill in Musick my self," he has views on the difficulties of men and birds in sharping a note!

Preluding Poor Richard in many ways as he does, Clayton, however, is not of rationalism all compact. He likes "remarkables" as well as any New Englander. A woman suffering from the gripes [13] had her torments increase as the thunderclouds approached closer, and "the Thunder there is attended often with fatal circumstances: I was with my Lord *Howard* of

[13] Clayton's vivid description is worth recording: ". . . the Distemper of the Colick that is predominant & has miserable sad effects it begins with violent gripes wch declineing takes away the use of limbs their fingers stand stifly bent the hands of some hang as if they were loose at the wrists from the arms, they are scelatons so meager & leane that a consumption might seeme a fatning to them" (letter to Nehemiah Grew [?] from Jamestown, April 24, 1684, *William and Mary College Quarterly,* 2d ser., I [1921], 114).

Effingham the Governour, when they brought word" that a doctor had been killed while smoking his pipe. Often the air had "a perfect Sulphureous Smell." A cold spring on my Lady Berkeley's property had "fatal Consequences to several," apparently by freezing their visceral organs. Flatly denying that snakeroot cures a rattlesnake bite, he was yet capable of writing about the beavers:

[They] are very subtil Creatures, and if half of the Stories be true that I have been told, they have a very Orderly Government amongst them; in their Works each knows his proper Work, and Station, and the Overseers beat those Young Ones that loiter in their Business, and will make them cry, and work stoutly (XVIII, 124–125).

He continually insists that if he had not lost all his books, microscope, and instruments by shipwreck, he would have rendered more exact descriptions than those written from memory, which "may be liable to Mistakes, and yet the Sincerity of the Person that delivers them intire," but it is a little difficult to believe that memory alone gave him so exact a description as the following:

There be frequent little sorts of Whirl-winds, whose Diameter may be sometimes not past two or three Yards, sometimes Forty, which whisking round in a Circle, pass along the Earth, according to the Motion of the Cloud, from whence they issue; and as they pass along with their gyrous or circular Motion, they carry aloft the drie Leaves into the Air, which fall again often in places far remote. I have seen them descend in a calm Sun-shine Day, as if they had come from the Heavens in great Showers thereof, so that all the Elements seem'd filled therewith. And I could perceive them to descend from on high as far as I could possibly discern a Leaf. I remember a roguish Expression of a Seaman, otherwise silly enough, who wondering thereat, cry'd out, *Sure now 'tis manifest there is a World above!* and now with them 'tis the Fall of the Leaf (XVII, 789).

This is good writing, obviously dependent upon careful notes, but its goodness is the goodness of utility, the large discourse of the earlier part of the century having vanished. Yet with all his crotchets, Clayton was humble before the mighty presence of nature: "I cannot think any thing too difficult or wonderful for Nature," he says, having in mind "Nature's Curiosity, in every thing." And because the planters blunder in their employment of nature, because they waste the resources of Virginia, the fussy little clergyman is on fire to reform their ways and reorganize their economy:

No Country in the World can be more curiously watered. But this Conveniency, that in future times may make her like the *Netherlands,* the richest place in all *America,* at the present I look on the greatest Impediment to the Advance of the Country, as it is the greatest Obstacle to Trade and Commerce. For the great number of Rivers and the thinness of the Inhabitants distract and disperse a Trade. . . . The best of Trade that can be driven is only a sort of *Scotch* Pedling (XVII, 791–792).

Thus their Plantations run over vast Tracts of Ground, each ambitioning to engross as much as they can, that they may be sure to have enough to Plant, and for their Stocks and Herds of Cattle to range and feed in, that Plantations of 1000, 2000, or 3000 Acres are common, whereby the Country is thinly inhabited; their Living solitary and unsociable; Trading confused and dispersed; besides other Inconveniences (XVII, 979).

How Clayton proposed to remedy these "Inconveniences" his letters testify.

The great subject of later Virginia literature in the seventeenth century was Bacon's Rebellion, to the literature of which some brief attention to one or two pamphlets primarily of economic interest will serve as an appropriate prelude. To be sure, the political upheavals of the period had their profound effects upon the public life of the colony, but historians of the rebellion are now agreed in finding economic tensions at the bottom of the political and social division between small planters and great, frontiersmen and tidewater aristocrats, democratically minded commoners and royalists of the governing class. Indeed, the economic theme perhaps bulks larger in the history of the time than it does in the literature, but at least a few treatises which propose the economic betterment of Virginia fall within the purlieus of literature.

To one who has read extensively in earlier promotion literature *A Perfect Description of Virginia* (1649) [14] has little that is new. Its fifty-seven numbered paragraphs enumerate the commodities, industries, population, etc., of the commonwealth, the chief novelties being a plea for iron furnaces and workers, an enumeration of existing wind and water mills, and paragraphs on silk culture and on the culture of the vine. Under Berkeley, it appears, "they in *Virginia* shall be as happie a people as any under heaven, for

[14] *A Perfect Description of Virginia: being, A full and true Relation of the present State of the Plantation . . . Being sent from Virginia, at the request of a Gentleman of worthy note . . . also, A Narration of the Countrey . . . With the Manner how the Emperor Nichotowance came to Sir William Berckley* (London, 1649); reprinted in Force, *Tracts,* Vol. II, no. 8. Quotations are from the Force edition.

there is nothing wanting there to produce them, *Plenty, Health,* and *Wealth.*" These objects are of importance to E. Williams' pamphlet of 1650, *Virginia: More especially the South part thereof, Richly and truly valued,*[15] which anticipated, or occasioned, a much more "literary" document, and which, because it has North Carolina mostly in view, is not here discussed. But *The Reformed Virginian Silk-Worm* of 1655,[16] a strange, disorderly catchall, has greater literary importance and more immediate point. The naïf charm of the various prose units which compose this queer little piece has not disappeared:

By burning of all kinde of Woods and Gums, you'le soon finde by your nose what sweet Perfumes they yield. And by the ponderousness or weight of earths, you may know if Minerals or not? Let it be known also, if you have not Waters of more than ordinary

[15] The second edition was "with Addition of The Discovery of Silkworms with their benefit. And Implanting of Mulberry Trees. Also The Dressing of Vines, for the rich Trade of making Wines in Virginia. Together with The making of the Saw-mill, very useful in Virginia, for cutting of Timber and Clapboard," and is reprinted in the Force *Tracts,* Vol. III, no. 11.

[16] The full title is almost necessary for an understanding of the pamphlet: *The Reformed Virginian Silk-Worm, Or, a Rare and New Discovery of A speedy way, and easie means, found out by a young Lady in England, she having made full proof thereof in May, Anno 1652. For the feeding of Silk-worms in the Woods, on the Mulberry-Tree-leaves in Virginia: Who after fourty dayes time, present their most rich golden-coloured silken Fleece, to the instant wonderful enriching of all the Planters there, requiring from them neither cost, labour, or hindrance in any of their other employments whatsoever. And also to the good hopes, that the Indians, seeing and finding that there is neither Art, Skill, or Pains in the thing: they will readily set upon it, being by the benefit thereof inabled to buy of the English (in way of Truck for their Silk-bottoms) all those things that they most desire* (London, 1655); reprinted in the Force *Tracts,* Vol. III, no. 13, from which quotations are made.

qualities; for taste, colours, smell, weight, hotness, or coldness? there is much depends upon them. And you shall know if they proceed out of any Minerals, by taking a glass full, and putting into it a Gall beaten to powder, which will turn the water into a reddish colour: and send samples of all kinde of strange earths, and of all other kinde of things without fail (p. 24).

More striking, however, is the verse with which the whole concludes. Struggling with rhyme and meter, "I. F." (John Ferrar?) manages, with characteristic American brag, to inform even the unpoetical that worms in Virginia grow enormously better than those of Europe:

> Worms are huge whose bottoms dare
> With Lemmons of the largest size compare.
> And twenty one of ours will sure poize less
> Then one of theirs for weight and ponderousness.
>   .   .   .   .   .   .
> Her dainty coloured flies and large Worms
> In length and bigness do surpass mens Thumbs.
> Whereas ours short of little fingers come.

Eggs that take nine months to hatch in Europe hatch in nine days in Virginia; and the enthusiasm of the propagandist paints an exquisitely ludicrous picture of Virginia woods hung all over with cocoons:

> Non-parrel *Virginia* in her Woods,
> Brings forth as all men know these precious goods:
> Where thousand fleeces fit for Princes Robes
> On Virgin-trees shall hang in Silken Globes.
> The noble Worm so hardy, stong [*sic*] and stout
> No weather ill is able them to rout.

Though the verse could be bettered, it must be said that the enthusiasm for silkworms on the part of Samuel Hartlib, John Ferrar, various anonymous or initialed gentlemen, and the shadowy lady named Virginia whose experiments occasioned this queer document arose from a praiseworthy determination to correct the imbalance of a colony overly given to tobacco growing and without a single city. A similar analysis lies at the bottom of the vigorous and workmanlike pamphlet by "R. G.," entitled *Virginia's Cure* (1662),[17] which attempts the wellnigh impossible feat of proving that religion requires Christians to live together in cities.

Whatever the value of these vagaries to modern eyes, economic theorizing was swept out of the land by the unprecedented and dramatic struggle we know as Bacon's Rebellion, which ran its course in 1675 and 1676 and which occasioned the richest library of original historical narratives coming out of Virginia during the period.[18] Without any historiographical theorizing and having in view only the pragmatical necessity of rendering an account to English officials or of writing down some passionate *ex parte* statement, this material, even when crude and awkward, lives. Who touches this book, said Whitman, touches a man. Who touches the literature of Bacon's Rebellion feels the very pulsebeat of the time. Thus the wife of the great rebel informs her sister:

[17] London, 1662; reprinted in the Force *Tracts,* Vol. III, no. 15.

[18] There are three excellent finding lists for this scattered material: (a) "List of Manuscript Sources for Bacon's Rebellion Which Have been Printed," *Virginia Magazine of History and Biography,* XIV (1907), 296–301; (b) "Original Sources of Information," in Mary Newton Stanard, *The Story of Bacon's Rebellion* (New York and Washington, 1907), pp. 171–181; (c) "Essay on Authorities" (the only critical discussion), in Thomas J. Wertenbaker, *Torchbearer of the Revolution: The Story of Bacon's Rebellion and Its Leader* (Princeton, 1940), pp. 215–225. This last supersedes all other biographies of Nathaniel Bacon. There are various popular treatments.

The Govern[r] being very angry with him put out high things against him, and told mee that he would most certainly hang him as soon as hee returned, w[ch] hee would certainly have done; but what for fear of the Governour's hanging him, and what for fear of the Indians killing him brought mee to this sad condicon, but blessed be God hee came in very well, with the losse of a very few men; never was known such a fight in Virginia with so few men's losse.[19]

This is not literature; it is, however, epical humanity. Bacon himself was a compelling orator, whose speeches, though they have often come down to us through the pens of his enemies, have the succinct Roman ring to them, as when he "faced his little army of tired, hungry, ragged men, in the depths of the Virginia forest" and spoke thus:

Gentlemen, the indefatigable pains we have taken deserve better success than we have met with. But there is nothing that cannot be accomplished by labor and industry, which makes me hope we may yet meet the heathen to square accounts for their barbarous cruelties done us. I should rather my body should lie rotting in the woods and never again see an Englishman's face, than fail in this service which the country expects of me and I vowed to perform against these heathen. Should I return without having punished and intimidated them, they would be as much animated as the English discouraged. My enemies would seize the opportunity to insult me and misrepresent me, saying that my defense of the country is a mere pretense to cloak other designs. But that all may see how devoted I am to our cause, I am determined to go on with any who will follow me, even though we have to undergo

[19] Mrs. Nathaniel Bacon to her sister (in England), June 29, 1676, *William and Mary College Quarterly*, 1st ser., IX (1901), 5.

the worst hardships of this wilderness, if need be subsisting on nuts and horseflesh. Therefore I shall set my standard outside the camp, so that those who wish to remain can rally around it. The rest have free leave to return to their homes.[20]

Herein one overhears the anticipation of the rolling periods and Augustan eloquence of the American Revolution.[21] Even a Mr. John Goode, not otherwise suspected of artistic interest, reporting a dialogue between Bacon and himself, reaches a certain dramatic insight. "Sir," said Goode, "you speake as though you had design'd a totall defection from Majestie, and our native Country." Bacon: "Why (smiling) haue not many Princes lost their Dominions soe." Goode, who seems to have had cynical insight, represents himself as then telling the rebel general:

They haue been such people as haue been able to subsist without their Prince. The poverty of Virginia is such, that the Major part of the Inhabitants can

[20] Quoted in Wertenbaker, *Torchbearer,* p. 149, who has, however, modernized the original.

[21] Aside from a lack of control over sentence structure, note how the rhetoric of eighteenth-century revolutionary documents is anticipated in Bacon's proclamations: e.g., "Wee appeale to the Country itselfe what and of what nature their Oppressions have bin or by what Caball and mistery the designes of many of those whom wee call great men have bin transacted and caryed on, but let us trace these men in Authority and Favour by whose hands the dispensation of the Countries wealth has been commited; let us observe the sudden Rise of their Estates composed [compared?] with the Quality in wch they first entered this Country Or the Reputation they have held here amongst wise and discerning men, And lett us see wither their extractions and Education have not bin vile, And by what pretence of learning and vertue they could soe soon [enter] into Imployments of so great Trust and consequence" (*Virginia Magazine of History and Biography,* I [1893], 56). The "Declaration of the People" which follows enumerates the crimes and abuses of Berkeley and his friends in a fashion anticipatory of the Declaration of Independence.

scarce supply their wants from hand to mouth, and many there are besides can hardly shift, without Supply one yeare, and you may bee sure that this people which soe fondly follow you, when they come to feele the miserable wants of food and rayment, will bee in greater heate to leave you, then they were to come after you, besides here are many people in Virginia that receive considerable benefitts, comforts, and advantages by Parents, Friends and Correspondents in England, and many which expect patrimonyes and Inheritances which they will by no meanes decline.[22]

Sociological analysis can scarcely be more compact.

Out of the swarm of letters, proclamations, counterproclamations, complaints, appeals, petitions, lists of grievances, and the like huge paper detritus left behind by this profound social convulsion, some halfdozen accounts emerge as being especially touched by literary art. These are:

T. M. [Thomas Mathews] *The Beginning, Progress, and Conclusion of Bacon's Rebellion in Virginia, In the Years 1675 and 1676.*[23]

Virginias Deploured Condition. Or an Impartiall Narrative of the Murders committed by the Indians there, and of the Sufferings of his Ma[ties]

---

[22] George Brown Goode, *Virginia Cousins* (Richmond, 1887), pp. 30B–30D. The "Dialogue between the Rebel Bacon and One Goode as it was Presented to the Right Honorable Sir Wm. Berkeley, Governor of Virginia" is here reprinted from "Colonial Entry Book, Vol. LXXI, pp. 232–240."

[23] Written in 1705 at the request of Robert Harley, this manuscript remained in the Harleian library, was bought in 1801 by Rufus King in London and sent by him in 1803 to Jefferson. It was first printed in the Richmond *Enquirer,* September 1, 5, 8, 1804, and has been reprinted in the *Virginia Evangelical and Literary Magazine,* III (1820), 128–149; the Force *Tracts,* Vol. I, no. 8; the *Virginia Historical Register and Literary Note Book,* III (1850), 61–75, 121–136; and Charles M. Andrews, ed., *Narratives of the Insurrections, 1675–*

Loyall Subiects vnder the Rebellious outrages of Mr Nathaniell Bacon Junr: to the tenth day of August A. Dom 1676.[24]
The Burwell Papers.[25]

1690 (New York, 1915), pp. 15–41. Quotations in the text, however, are from the Force *Tracts.*

[24] Printed among the Aspinwall Papers in *Coll. Mass. Hist. Soc.,* 4th ser., IX (1871), 162–176.

[25] This document and the next still remain mysterious, and the connection between them has never been satisfactorily explained:

(a) The so-called Burwell Papers were first printed (inaccurately) from manuscript furnished Josiah Quincy by William A. Burwell of Virginia, the covering letter being dated Washington, December 20, 1812. This was in *Coll. Mass. Hist. Soc.,* 2d ser., I (1814), 27–80. This material was then reprinted in the Force *Tracts,* Vol. I, no. 11. Following some dispute as to the ownership of the manuscript and discovering "numerous errors of orthography and punctuation, besides other still more important; the whole number of errata amounting to several thousands," the assistant librarian reprinted the material (correctly) in *Proc. Mass. Hist. Soc., 1866–67,* IX (1867), 298–342, and from this version quotations in the text are made. Entitled "The History of Bacon's and Ingram's Rebellion, 1676," this was reprinted in C. M. Andrews, *op. cit.,* pp. 47–98.

(b) The "Mrs. An. Cotton" *Account of Our Late Troubles,* which is in the form of a letter to one "Mr. C. H. at Yardly in Northamptonshire," was first printed in the Richmond *Enquirer,* September 12, 1804, and thence reprinted in the Force *Tracts,* Vol. I, no. 9. A good deal of ingenuity has been expended in the effort to identify "Mrs. An. Cotton" and "Mr. C. H.," the results being admirably summed up in J. B. Hubbell's article, "John and Ann Cotton of 'Queen's Creek,' Virginia," *American Literature,* X (1938–39), 179–201. Mr. Hubbell thinks that John Cotton wrote the "narrative," his wife Ann, the "letter," and assumes that Mrs. Cotton wrote the shorter manuscript for Mr. "C. H." because Cotton had no copy of his longer narrative to send or because the "narrative" gave too favorable an account of Bacon—an inference drawn from the fact that the "Mrs. An. Cotton" material does not include Bacon's epitaph. Mr. Hubbell, however, argues on pp. 186–188 that John Cotton wrote both the epitaph and the reply to the epitaph, so that this inference would seem to fall to the ground. He seems also to confuse Ann Graves Cotton, wife of William Cotton (the *father* of John Cotton) and Hannah Cotton, wife of John Cotton.

That "Mrs. An. Cotton" and "Mr. C. H." are real persons is of

An Account of Our Late Troubles in Virginia. Written in 1676, by Mrs. An. Cotton, of Q. Creeke.

[John Berry and Francis Moryson], *A True Narrative of the Rise, Progresse, and Cessation of the Late Rebellion in Virginia, Most Humbly and Impartially Reported by his Majestyes Commissioners Appointed to Enquire into the Affairs of the said Colony.*[26]

Strange News from Virginia. Being a full and true

---

course possible. The ostensible occasion of "Mrs. Cotton's" letter is, however, suspicious, inasmuch as another letter to an anonymous person, whose permission to write starts off "Mrs. Cotton" offers a preliminary barrier strongly suggestive of the apparition of Mrs. Veal. Moreover, the assumption that "An." necessarily means "Ann" or "Anne" is sheer assumption; it may be an abbreviated form of a masculine name, like "Anas." (Cf. Anas Todkill of earlier fame.) More curious still is the relation between the "Mrs. An. Cotton" material and the Burwell narrative. The author of the "Mrs. An. Cotton" material has lifted out of the Burwell narrative a reference to Scogan's *Jest Book,* a series of metaphors drawn from cardplaying, millstones, cripples and wild animals, and various other phrases scarcely suggesting a feminine pen. In sum, the "Mrs. An. Cotton" letter is plainly derivative, as if an inexperienced writer, presumably a man, were struggling with a task of literary condensation too difficult for him. A final letter from "Mr. Cotton" concludes the "Mrs. An. Cotton" material, but this letter is vague in origin ("From Towne, June 9, '76") and is not a letter from a living husband to a living wife, but simply two highly rhetorical paragraphs about fortune and the fall of Bacon. The guess may be hazarded, despite Mr. Hubbell's able paper, that Virginia never saw a gifted literary woman named "Mrs. An. Cotton," but that, for some reason now unknown, some literary hack or even some person without literary training found it profitable to condense awkwardly the Burwell material. But see C. E. Schorer, " 'One Cotton of Acquia Creek, Husband of Ann Cotton,' " *American Literature,* XXII (1950), 342–345, for a contrary point of view.

[26] Originally published in *Virginia Magazine of History and Biography,* IV (1896), 117–154 (from which the quotations in the text are taken) and reprinted in C. M. Andrews, *op. cit.,* pp. 105–141. Although the commission was composed of Colonel Herbert Jeffreys, John Berry, and Colonel Francis Moryson, only the last two signed the document.

Account of the Life and Death of Nathaniel Bacon, Esquire. (London, 1677.)[27]

Of these six documents the last is least important both in substance and in style. None of these accounts, it should be noted, is primarily by a "Baconian," and one of the tributes to this remarkable leader is the reluctant admiration wrung from his enemies and investigators.

The narrative of Thomas Mathews, written up from notes (one guesses) some thirty years after the event, is that of a not unsympathetic spectator forced against his will to participate in events he disapproved. Fearful of "those pernicious entanglem'ts in the labyrinths and snares of state ambiguities," he was compelled to serve as Bacon's secretary, and his timorousness peeps through a conscientious, if awkward, narrative. He tells what he knows and what he learned from others, but his best endeavors to explain why the commotion arose are to enumerate three prodigies—a comet, endless flights of pigeons, and swarms of flies "about an inch long, and big as the top of a man's little finger," baleful omens for the year 1675. His herdsman was killed by Indians and "from this Englishman's bloud did (by degrees) arise Bacons rebellion with the following mischiefs which overspread all Virginia and twice endangered Maryland"—scarcely a profound diagnosis. We owe to the appendix of his narrative, however, one suggestion of startling significance; namely that Richard Lawrence, the wealthy planter, played Mephistopheles to Bacon's Faust. Bacon was, says Mathews,

[27] This item, together with *More News from Virginia* (London, 1677) has been reprinted by Harry Firestone as *Bacon's Rebellion: The Contemporary News Sheets* (Charlottesville, 1956).

too young, too much a stranger there, and of a disposition too precipitate, to manage things to that length those were carried, had not thoughtful Mr. Lawrence been at the bottom (p. 26).

A temperamental conservative,[28] Mathews in his timid way nevertheless manages three or four dramatic bits—Bacon on his knees before Berkeley "confessing" his crimes, Berkeley's savage comment: "Mr. Drumond! you are very welcome, I am more glad to see you, than any man in Virginia, Mr. Drumond you shall be hang'd in half an hour," King Charles's comment on the half-mad governor: "that old fool has hang'd more men in that naked country, than he had done for the murther of his ffather." But the vividness is spotty, the account lacks any determinate point of view, and we put it down respecting Bacon but not respecting Thomas Mathews.

The venom of *Virginias Deploured Condition* leaves no doubt where lie the sympathies of its author or authors; and if doubt existed, it would end before the climax of the tale:

Thus is that Country by the rashness of a *p*'uerce [perverse] man expoased to ruin, and is in a most calamitious & confused condicon, lyeing open to the cruelty of the saluage Indians, who in all likelyhood had before now beene totally subiected had not an insulting rabble prevented, who account the Law their manacles, and like swine turne all into disorder & become insolent, abuse all in authority (as a comon drunkard being lately comitted to the stocks thretned the Magistrate to raise a Mutiny) throwing off all allegience to his most sacred Ma.ᵗʸ and the Crowne

[28] It is, he thinks, a "convincing proofe against infidelity" that the Indian king's son, being baptized, took nourishment when ill, which he would not do before.

of England, and dareingly say they will have the dutch to trade thither, with such like expressions (p. 176).

The swelling anger of the conservative shaken by fright informs the account, which, amidst all of his abuse of Bacon and his followers, manages to retain a certain dignity and conviction of style.

It has already been indicated that the *Account of Our Late Troubles in Virginia* by "Mrs. An. Cotton" derives from the Burwell Papers and need not therefore require independent discussion. This fact leaves two works of major importance, one of which has been sadly damaged by time. But although the tattered fragments of the Burwell account begin abruptly with the tag end of a sentence, though their later pages run into the sands of conjecture and lost phrases, the three parts of this history—"The Indians Proseedings," "Bacons Proseedings," "Ingrams Proseedings"—are stylistically the most interesting work written in the period and offer a curious pendant to *The Simple Cobler of Aggawam.* Their author was a seventeenth-century humorist after the manner of Tom Brown and his ilk, mingling pedantry and puns, extravagant metaphors and unexpected flippancies, invented words and fantastic paralogisms like a Virginian Rabelais. He has read *Scoggan's Jests* and the *Resolves* of Owen Feltham, Thomas Fuller, and the Iliad; he refers to the Koran, *Reynard the Fox,* Scanderberg, Euphues, "Bellonies Bagpipe" and "Marsses whisle," the Copernican theory, "the hoggs the devill sheard," the fables of Æsop, the astrolabe, three essential properties of a general, and the titmouse which became an elephant. Everything is bathed in the same atmosphere of levity; and though in general the narrative is anti-Bacon, the author does not trouble to conceal his own cynical interpretation of the upper-class attitude towards the general "by the consent of ye people":

> They began (som of them) to haue Bacons Merits in mistrust, as a Luminary that thretned an eclips to there riseing gloryes. For though he was but a yong man, yet they found that he was master and owner of those induments which constitutes a Compleate Man, (as to intrincecalls) wisdom to apprehend and descretion to chuse. By which imbelishments (if he should continue in the Governours favour) of Seniours they might becom juniors, while there yoñger Brother, through the nimbleness of his wit, might steale away that blessing, which they accounted there owne by birthright. This rash proseedings of Bacon, if it did not undo himselfe, by his faileing in the enterprise, might chance to undo them in the affections of the people; which to prevent, they thought it conduceable to there intress and establishment, for to get yᵉ Governour in the minde to proclame him a Rebell; as knowing that once being don, since it could not be don but by and in the Governours name, it must needs breed bad blodd betwene Bacon and Sʳ William, not easely to be purged (p. 304).

This is straight cynicism; the levity with which the author describes tragic events is evident in his description of the death of Col. Hansford, trapped by Berkeley's men in "the Temple of Venus"—"the last Sacryfize he ever after offred at the Shrine of that Luxurious Deity, for . . . he had the ill luck to be the first Verginian borne that dyed upon a paire of Gallows." [29] His disgust with Berkeley, however, is even

[29] Cf. his comment on the hanging of Captain Farlow: "This man was much pittied by those who were aquainted with him, as one of a peacable dispossition, had a good scholer, which one might thinke

deeper than his distrust of Bacon, as is evident from
the cold distaste of a celebrated incident in his story:

When that the Major [Cheeseman] was brought
in to the Governor⁵ presence, and by him demanded,
what made him to ingage in Bacons designes? Before
that the Major could frame an Answer, to the Gov-
ernours demand; his Wife steps in and tould his honʳ,
that it was her provocations that made her Husband
joyne in the Cause that Bacon contended for; ading,
that if he had not bin influenc'd by her instigations, he
had never don that which he had don. Therefore
(upon her bended knees) she desired of his hon.ʳ,
that since what her Husband had don, was by her
meanes, and so, by Consequence, she most guilty, that
shee might be hang'd, and he pardon'd. Though the
Governour did know, that what she had saide, was
neare to the truth, yet he saide litle to her request,
onely telling of her that she was a W———. But his
hon.ʳ was angrey, & therefore this expression must be
interprited the efects of his passion, not his meane-
ing: For it is to be understood in reason, that there is
not any Woman, who hath soe small affection, for her
Husband, as to dishonour him by her dishonisty, and
yet retaine such a degree of love, that rather then he
should be hang'd, shee will be content to submit her
owne life to the Sentance, to keep her husband from
yᵉ Gallows (p. 328).

The brutality of the generalization in these circumstances is an obvious *reprise* for the brutality dis-
played by the governor.

In truth, our author is a libertine philosopher of
the cynic school, in whom the extravagances of parti-

---

should haue inabled him to have taken a better estimate of his im-
ployment, as he was äquainted with the Mathamaticks: But it seems
the Asstrolabe, or Quadrant, are not the fitest instruments to take the
altitude of a Subjects duty; the same being better demonstrated by
practicall, not Speculatiue observations" (p. 329).

sans arouse either amusement or disdain. Bacon's is an "Al-a-mode Rebellion," he frightens the people with "this Bugbeare," his successor is a "Milk-sopp Generall," a peacock on a dunghill, an ape coming after the death of the lion. One of his officers is a "Whisker of Whorley-Giggs," whose station as a miller sets off a whole train of uncomplimentary metaphors. Another keeps a Negro mistress, "as though Venus was cheifely to be worshiped in the Image of a Negro: or that Buty consisted all together in the Antiphety of Complections," but what would you? "If Sʳ Williams Cause were no better then his fortunes, hither to, how many prossellites might his disasters bring over to the tother side?" Men's fortunes are compared to a game of cards, a corn between millstones; Indians are "Wolves, Tygers, and Foxis" which daily prey on sheep and lambs.

And here who can do less than wonder at the muteable and impermenent deportments of that blinde Godes Fortune; who, in the morning loades Man with disgraces, and ere night crownes him with honours: Sometimes depressing, and againe ellivateing, as her fickle humer is to smile or frowne, of which this Genᵗ:mans fate was a kinde of an Eppittemey, in the severall vicissetudes and changes he was subjected to in a very few dayes (pp. 305–306).

If the modern historian finds deep, prophetical significance in Bacon's Rebellion, this writer, despite his grudging admiration for that general, found no meaning in these garboils, except a certain intellectual delight in the skill with which "Bacon knit more knotts by his owne head in one day, then all the hands in Towne was able to untye in a wholl weeke."

And yet, whether the world "stand still with Ptoll-

omye, or turne rownd like a whorlegigg with Co-
pernicus," our author cannot stifle his pleasure in
Nathaniel Bacon, who, at the end, "surrendred up
that Fort he was no longer able to keepe, into the
hands of that grim and all conquering Captaine,
Death."

It must be confest that he was a Gent:man of a
Liberall education, and so consequently must be re-
plenish'd with good maners, which inables, and oblig-
eth all civell parsons [persons] both to remember,
and repay, receued curtesces (p. 322);

and though the intent of the passage (in its context)
is sarcastic, a hundred little touches show that Bacon
was a better gentleman than Sir William Berkeley
and that the author of the Burwell narrative was uneasy and ashamed before the fact. For it is to him
that we owe the preservation of the famous "Epitaph, made by his Man," the most famous piece of
poetry to come out of seventeenth-century Virginia.
("There was many coppes of Vercēs made after his
departure," he says surlily, "calculated to the Latti-
tude of there affections who composed them.")

Death why soe crewill! what no other way
To manifest thy splleene, but thus to slay
Our hopes of safety; liberty, our all
Which, through thy tyrany, with him must fall
To its late Caoss? Had thy riged force
Bin delt by retale, and not thus in gross
Griefe had bin silent . . . .
    If't bee a sin to thinke Death brib'd can bee
Wee must be guilty; say twas bribery
Guided the fatall shaft. Verginias foes,
To whom for secrit crimes, just vengeance owes
Disarved plagues, dreding their just disart
Corrupted Death by Parasscellcian art

Him to destroy . . . .
Marss and *Minerva,* both in him Concurd
For arts, for arms, whose pen and sword alike,
As *Catos* did, may admireation strike
In to his foes; while they confess with all
It was there guilt stil'd him a Criminall.
. . . . .
Here let him rest; while wee this truth report
He's gon from hence unto a higher Court
To pleade his Cause: where he by this doth know
WHETHER TO CEASER HEE WAS FRIEND, OR FOE (pp.
323–324).

Then, after copying out this sonorous tribute, the author, as if to conceal his emotion and ostensibly hold
the balance even, prints "Vpon the Death of G:B,"
a spirited defamation, which, beginning with the last
line of the preceding poem, proceeds in a crescendo
of attack to an ending worthy of Dryden:

And what no Baile could save
He hath commited Prissoner to the Grave;
From whence there's no repreive. Death keep him
close
Wee have too many Divells still goe loose.[30]

If the Burwell narrative, with its *facetiae,* shows
that even in Virginia the latest styles in seventeenth-
century prose were worn, the *True Narrative* signed
by John Berry and Francis Moryson, clear, efficient,
cool-headed, and not too unjust, anticipates the lucid-

[30] The inference to be drawn from every comparison of style, man-
agement of meter, allusion, and structure of these two poems is that
they are the products of the same pen, and should in all probability
be viewed as rhetorical exercises defending and attacking Bacon
probably with a view to concealing the real sympathies of the author
of the Burwell narrative. That the epitaph was really by Bacon's
"man" and that a second writer immediately seized upon it, made
the last line the occasion of a second poem of equal excellence, and so
gave the colony two unknown Miltons is slightly incredible.

ity of eighteenth-century work. "The Particulars of
this . . . Narrative," they remark,

being what wee could collect or observe from the most
credible disinterest'd Persons, most authentique Papers, Records, Reports and the Publick Grievances of
the respective countyes of Virginia, wee have, with
all integrity of mind and the best of our understanding, without favor or partiality, selected and sett
downe what wee thought most consonant to Truth &
Reality, and on the other hand rejected whatever wee
found or suspected to be false or improbable (p.
154).

The sympathies of the commissioners were not with
the populace,[31] but they were reasonable men who
soon learned that Berkeley had no monopoly of truth:
"The unsatisfied People finding themselves still lyable
to the Indian Crueltyes, and the cryes of their wives
and children growing grievous and intollerable to
them," they could under that "among the Vulgar it
matters not whether they be Friends or Foes Soe they
be Indians." They paint in swift strokes the principal
events, employing a compact, narrative style for the
purpose, of which the following is a typical sentence:

The Indians persisting to Revenge themselves In-
forted in Maryland and now began to be bold and
formidable to the English who Besieged them; their
Boldness and daring behavior of late tymes and
their promptnesse to Fire arms, being (indeed) won-
derfull, over what they seem'd formerly, indued with
which doubtlesse was of some advantage extraordinary to them considering their Small Body (p. 119).

[31] "Thus the sense of this oppression and the dread of a comon approaching calamity made the giddy-headed multitude madd, and
precipitated them upon that rash overture of Running out upon the
Indians themselves, at their owne voluntary charge and hazard of
their Lives and Fortunes" (p. 121).

We owe to their insight the best character sketch of
Bacon to be found in all this material:

> Hee was a person whose erratique fortune had car-
> ryed and shewne him many Forraigne Parts, and of
> no obscure Family. Upon his first comming into Vir-
> ginia hee was made one of the Councill, the reason of
> that advancement (all on a suddain) being best
> known to the Governour, which honor made him the
> more considerable in the eye of the Vulgar, and gave
> some advantage to his pernicious designes. Hee was
> said to be about four or five and thirty yeares of age,
> indifferent tall but slender, blackhair'd and of an omi-
> nous, pensive, melancholly Aspect, of a pestilent &
> prevalent Logical discourse tending to atheisme in
> most companyes, not given to much talke, or to make
> suddain replyes, of a most imperious and dangerous
> hidden Pride of heart, despising the wisest of his
> neighbours for their Ignorance, and very ambitious
> and arrogant. But all these things lay hidd in him till
> after hee was a councillor, and untill he became pow-
> erfull & popular (p. 122).

This is a hostile portrait, but it is not malicious; and
the commissioners are capable of justifying some of
Bacon's military measures, like the hanging of James
Wilkinson, "which (as a soldier) wee look on to be
more an act of his Policy than cruelty, to prevent and
awe others from disserting him, wee not observing
him to have bin Bloodely inclined in the whole progresse of this Rebellion." Moreover, the conduct of
the governor's party, though it might fight for right-
eousness, aroused little enthusiasm in the commision-
ers: "soe great was the Cowardize and Basenesse of
the Generality of Sr. William Berkeley's Party (being most of them men intent onely upon plunder or
compell'd and hired into his service)" they say in one
place; and in another: "But the maine service that

was done for the reducing the Rebells to their obe-
dience was done by the Seamen and commanders of
Shipps then riding in the Rivers." As it was not the
purpose of the report to probe causes but to narrate
events, the lack of partisanship of the wrong sort and
the scope and range of the little history are a tribute
to the good sense of writers who, if they thought
Bacon and the populace were hideously wrong, were
not willing to follow Governor Berkeley into a frenzy
of insane vengefulness. For sheer narrative power
therefore this is one of the best pieces of the period.[32]
Although the number of items just surveyed could be
increased, enough has been shown to vindicate the
view that literature in and about Virginia in the first
century of its existence is richer and more varied than
much "literary" history has hitherto allowed. What
inferences can now be usefully drawn from this account? To what generalizations does it lead?

Overwhelmingly a literature of prose, the style of
this writing was in the main determined not by cultural elements in the colony but by the changing mode
in seventeenth-century England. Allowing for cultural
lag, one sees colonial prose slowly and awkwardly
transforming itself from the Elizabethan manner of

[32] *The Present State of Virginia and the College* by Henry Hart-
well, James Blair, and Edward Chilton, though written in 1697, was
not printed until 1727 and belongs to the eighteenth century. It was
edited and reprinted at Williamsburg by H. D. Farish in 1940. In
1964 Farish's edition was reprinted by the University Press of Virginia, Charlottesville, as a paperback in its Dominion Books series.
In "Virginia at the Close of the Seventeenth Century: An Appraisal
by James Blaire and John Locke," *Virginia Magazine of History and
Biography*, LXXIV (1966), 141–169, Michael G. Kammen argues
that a manuscript among the papers of John Locke, "Some of the
Cheif Greivances of the present constitution of Virginia, with an
Essay towards the Remedies thereof," is a collaborative effort by
Locke and Blair.

George Percy to the soberer style of the Berry-Mory-son *True Narrative* and the later legislative records. Even in the 1670's the facetiousness of the Burwell Papers has a belated air, and the future lies with a writer like William Fitzhugh or the Rev. John Clayton. In the next century the prose style of William Byrd II will bridge the gap between this literature and the Augustan manner of Washington and Thomas Jefferson.

Because Virginia writing was the monopoly of the governing class, acceptance of stylistic change, however backward, was rendered easier by the desire of the planter aristocracy to conform to the London mode. But the economic and social problems of the colony set up a barrier which screened out many fundamental elements in English prose of the seventeenth century. Virginia literature is lacking in introspection, in philosophic and moral meditation, in the subtle intellectual analysis which one associates with the sermons of Donne, the writings of Browne or Burton, the poetry of Milton, and the prose of Bunyan. It is a literature without theology—one of its principal differences from New England writing. It is, in truth, a literature without the play of general ideas, a theory of government being almost the sole philosophic problem it discusses. Economic speculation, to be sure, exists, but it is largely *ad hoc.*

What we have is a secular literature. It is oddly true that Virginia sermons are almost nonexistent but that the proportion of oratory is, as compared with the literature of New England, unusually high—the speeches of Smith, Powhatan, Berkeley, Bacon come at once to mind as being political and diplomatic rather than edifying or hortatory. For this literature the visible world exists. Its writers see and touch and taste and smell; they have themselves traveled into the woods, up the rivers; interrogated Indians; watched the rattlesnake, the red deer, the flying squirrel; fought against the Dutch or heard the frenzied speeches of Governor Berkeley. The vast American landscape has laid its spell upon them; and aside from one or two pieces in rhyme, they rise to poetry only when they seek to embody in words the fascination and terror of a boundless and lonely world.

Theirs is a pragmatic literature, a literature content with worldly values and worldly content, a literature which, as the period draws to its close, sets up the Horatian ideal of a just serenity as its aim. The writers are therefore perturbed by social disturbances in proportion as this peaceful aim is threatened. They take human nature easily, they are curious about personality, but they do not search character, for this would entail more effort than they care to expend. The world as it goes—this is enough for them. It is therefore, despite modern historical interpretations of Bacon's Rebellion, a literature fundamentally antidemocratic in value. From Percy and Smith to the Burwell Papers and the Berry-Moryson *Narrative* the Virginians believe in government by the wise and good, by those appointed or born to govern; and if they cry out now and again against the iniquities or the slothfulness of the gentlemen, it is not to overthrow aristocracy but to amend and freshen it. Authority must lodge somewhere—why not in the king, his representative, the council, the gentleman planters? For the sweaty multitude the writers have an almost Shakespearian disdain. The development of a more democratical literary spirit must await the eighteenth century.

INDEX OF PERSONS

*The Literature of Virginia
in the Seventeenth Century*

was composed, printed,
and bound by
Kingsport Press, Inc.,
Kingsport, Tennessee.
The types are Caslon,
Caslon Old Style,
and Caslon Open Face.
The paper is Warren's 1854.
Design is by Edward G. Foss.